New
Day

GW01019170

Edited by Naomi Starkey

~~~~~~~~~~ 2014

New Daylight © BRF 2014

The Bible Reading Fellowship
15 The Chambers, Vineyard, Abingdon OX14 3FE
Tel: 01865 319700; Fax: 01865 319701
E-mail: enquiries@brf.org.uk; Website: www.brf.org.uk

ISBN 978 0 85746 040 0

Distributed in Australia by Mediacom Education Inc., PO Box 610, Unley, SA 5061.
Tel: 1800 811 311; Fax: 08 8297 8719;
E-mail: admin@mediacom.org.au
Available also from all good Christian bookshops in Australia.
For individual and group subscriptions in Australia:
Mrs Rosemary Morrall, PO Box W35, Wanniassa, ACT 2903.

Distributed in New Zealand by Scripture Union Wholesale, PO Box 760, Wellington
Tel: 04 385 0421; Fax: 04 384 3990; E-mail: suwholesale@clear.net.nz

Publications distributed to more than 60 countries

Acknowledgments
The New Revised Standard Version of the Bible, Anglicised Edition, copyright © 1989, 1995 by
the Division of Christian Education of the National Council of the Churches of Christ in the
USA. Used by permission. All rights reserved.

The Holy Bible, New International Version, Anglicised edition, copyright © 1979, 1984, 2011
by Biblica (formerly International Bible Society). Used by permission of Hodder & Stoughton
Publishers, an Hachette UK company. All rights reserved. 'NIV' is a registered trademark of
Biblica (formerly International Bible Society). UK trademark number 1448790.

Extracts from the Authorised Version of the Bible (The King James Bible), the rights in which
are vested in the Crown, are reproduced by permission of the Crown's Patentee, Cambridge
University Press.

The Holy Bible, New Living Translation, copyright © 1996, 2004. Used by permission of
Tyndale House Publishers, Inc., Wheaton, Illinois 60189. All rights reserved.

The Good News Bible published by The Bible Societies/HarperCollins Publishers, copyright ©
1966, 1971, 1976, 1992 American Bible Society.

New King James Version of the Bible copyright © 1979, 1980, 1982 by Thomas Nelson, Inc.
All rights reserved.

The Revised Standard Version of the Bible, copyright © 1946, 1952, 1971 by the Division of
Christian Education of the National Council of the Churches of Christ in the United States of
America.

The Holy Bible, English Standard Version, published by HarperCollins Publishers © 2001
Crossway Bibles, a division of Good News Publishers. All rights reserved.

The New American Standard Bible® copyright © 1960, 1962, 1963, 1968, 1971, 1972, 1973,
1975, 1977, 1995 by The Lockman Foundation.

The New Testament in Modern English, Revised Edition, translated by J.B. Phillips. Copyright
© 1958, 1960, 1972 by J.B. Phillips.

The Revised Common Lectionary is copyright © The Consultation on Common Texts, 1992 and is
reproduced with permission. *The Christian Year: Calendar, Lectionary and Collects*, which includes
the *Common Worship* lectionary (the Church of England's adaptations of the *Revised Common
Lectionary*, published as the Principal Service lectionary) is copyright © The Central Board of
Finance of the Church of England, 1995, 1997, and material from it is reproduced with
permission.

Printed by Gutenberg Press, Tarxien, Malta.

Suggestions for using *New Daylight*

Find a regular time and place, if possible, where you can read and pray undisturbed. Before you begin, take time to be still and perhaps use the BRF prayer. Then read the Bible passage slowly (try reading it aloud if you find it over-familiar), followed by the comment. You can also use *New Daylight* for group study and discussion, if you prefer.

The prayer or point for reflection can be a starting point for your own meditation and prayer. Many people like to keep a journal to record their thoughts about a Bible passage and items for prayer. In *New Daylight* we also note the Sundays and some special festivals from the Church calendar, to keep in step with the Christian year.

New Daylight and the Bible

New Daylight contributors use a range of Bible versions, and you will find a list of the versions used opposite, on page 2. You are welcome to use your own preferred version alongside the passage printed in the notes. This can be particularly helpful if the Bible text has been abridged.

New Daylight affirms that the whole of the Bible is God's revelation to us, and we should read, reflect on and learn from every part of both Old and New Testaments. Usually the printed comment presents a straight-forward 'thought for the day', but sometimes it may also raise questions rather than simply providing answers, as we wrestle with some of the more difficult passages of Scripture.

New Daylight is also available in a deluxe edition (larger format). Visit your local Christian bookshop or contact the BRF office, who can also give details about a cassette version for the visually impaired. For a Braille edition, contact St John's Guild, 8 St Raphael's Court, Avenue Road, St Albans, AL1 3EH.

Comment on *New Daylight*

To send feedback, you may email or write to BRF at the addresses shown opposite. If you would like your comment to be included on our website, please email connect@brf.org.uk. You can also Tweet to @brfonline, using the hashtag #brfconnect.

Writers in this issue

Stephen Cottrell is the Bishop of Chelmsford. He has worked as Missioner in the Wakefield diocese and as part of Springboard, the Archbishop's evangelism team. His latest books are *From the Abundance of the Heart* (DLT, 2006) and *Do Nothing to Change Your Life* (CHP, 2007).

Veronica Zundel is an Oxford graduate, writer and journalist. She lives with her husband and son in North London, where they belong to the Mennonite Church.

Maggi Dawn is an author and theologian, currently based at Yale University, where she is Dean of Marquand Chapel and Associate Professor of Theology and Literature in the Divinity School.

Ian Adams is a writer and artist working with themes of spirituality, culture and community. He is co-director of the StillPoint project (www.thestillpoint.org.uk) and partner in the Beloved Life project. Ian is the creator of Morning Bell, a daily way into prayer (twitter.com/pacebene).

Michael Mitton is a freelance writer, speaker and consultant and the Fresh Expressions Adviser for the Derby Diocese. He is also the NSM Priest-in-charge of St Paul's Derby and honorary Canon of Derby Cathedral. He is the author of *Travellers of the Heart* (BRF, 2013).

Lakshmi Jeffreys as an Anglican priest, has served in parish ministry, university chaplaincy and as a mission officer across a diocese. She is involved in church leadership in a village just outside Northampton.

Naomi Starkey is a Commissioning Editor for BRF and edits and writes for *New Daylight* Bible reading notes. She has also written *The Recovery of Love* (BRF, 2012).

John Twisleton is parish priest of Horsted Keynes in West Sussex. He is the author of *Meet Jesus* (BRF, 2011) and broadcasts regularly on Premier Christian Radio.

Andy John has been the Bishop of Bangor since 2008, having previously served all his ministry in the Diocese of St Davids. He is married to Caroline, who is also a deacon in the Church in Wales.

Steve Aisthorpe lives in Scotland with his wife and two sons. He is a Mission Development Worker for the Church of Scotland, encouraging mission and discipleship throughout the Highlands and Islands. He was previously Executive Director of the International Nepal Fellowship.

Naomi Starkey writes...

In this final issue of *New Daylight*'s 'silver jubilee' year, it is interesting to look back to the momentous events of autumn 1989, 25 years ago, when the map of Europe was redrawn in a matter of weeks. No one who grew up during the Cold War is likely to forget the astonishing TV pictures of people singing and dancing on top of the Berlin Wall and the sense of 'history in the making' as regime after regime toppled in Eastern Europe.

Sadly, subsequent events, especially in the Balkans, showed that complex patterns of old alliances and old grievances could not be swept aside so easily. That tremendous season of change brought war and turmoil as well as hope and freedom—and the reminder that life is never a blank sheet of paper. We live, unavoidably, in the context of our personal stories, as well as the wider stories of our families, communities and nations.

Change takes time to process, even if it is, on balance, change for the better. It is tempting to want to rush to (and then linger at) the 'happy ending', but reality doesn't work like that. Surrounded by the loving care of God, we journey towards wholeness, but, while we will encounter seasons of special blessing along the way, we also need strength to face the inevitable times of pain and struggle.

It may be no coincidence that two contributors in this issue—Lakshmi Jeffreys and Maggi Dawn—have chosen to comment on the same story of Elijah (1 Kings 19:4–8). That story's message is of recuperation after an episode of fiery strife and breathtaking change. Elijah may have been a great servant of God but he still reached a point of total exhaustion. He still needed to be open to heavenly help.

Perhaps there is a gentle lesson here for any who are tempted to feel invincible but are actually in danger of burning out: look for the opportunities for rest and refreshment that God may be offering you. Perhaps there is consolation here for anyone feeling weary at the prospect of the change and commitments that the coming months will bring: God will grant you rest.

The BRF Prayer

Almighty God,
you have taught us that your word is a lamp for our feet
and a light for our path. Help us, and all who prayerfully
read your word, to deepen our fellowship with you
and with each other through your love.
And in so doing may we come to know you more fully,
love you more truly, and follow more faithfully
in the steps of your son Jesus Christ, who lives and reigns
with you and the Holy Spirit, one God for evermore.
Amen

Love and judgement: Hosea

Let us start near the end with what are probably Hosea's most famous verses: 'When Israel was a child', says the prophet, 'I loved him' (Hosea 11:1, NRSV).

Although this sizzling and challenging little book contains some of God's fiercest judgements, it is also the one in which the people of Israel seem to take a massive step forward in their understanding of who God is and how God relates to them. This God, who is also a God of judgement, to whom all things and all people must render account, is also a God of love. In fact they discover, albeit the hard way, that God's great love is the source of God's judgement. It is not that God is angry and sometimes he relents—God is always loving and always good and therefore always wants what is best. Therefore we find in this book an unfolding list of attitudes and behaviours that disappoint God and lead to wretchedness and judgement.

At the centre of the book, Hosea uses fairly shocking marital and sexual imagery as a metaphor for the relationship between God and those who follow him. Believers who are true to God are a chaste bride; those who are unfaithful are an adulterous prostitute. Hosea's life turns this metaphor into a living reality as God tells the prophet to marry a prostitute. Although the marriage of Hosea and Gomer provides the framework for the book, it is, of course, a prophetic word to the House of Israel for its waywardness and pursuit of idols. It is still very relevant for us today as we face the beguiling snares of many idols and seek to live faithful lives.

Hosea wrote in the eighth century before Christ—a time of violent upheaval. Israel was split between two kingdoms with two rival temples. Successive prophets—notably, in the north, Hosea and Amos—warn of the consequences of abandoning God's way. Eventually Israel is overthrown by Assyria. We therefore read Hosea against the backdrop of this impending doom. We also note that Hosea's beautiful imagery of God's faithfulness to the people he loves continues to have a huge influence on Christian thinking about God today.

Stephen Cottrell

A wife of whoredom

When the Lord first spoke through Hosea, the Lord said to Hosea, 'Go, take for yourself a wife of whoredom and have children of whoredom, for the land commits great whoredom by forsaking the Lord.' So he went and took Gomer daughter of Diblaim, and she conceived and bore him a son.

Many of the prophets were called to live out on behalf of God's people the hardships and deprivations that they were bringing on themselves, so that they would see where their own behaviour was leading. Only Hosea is given such a disturbing and shocking vocation, however: so that Israel may learn the consequences of its own unfaithfulness, Hosea is asked to take a prostitute as his wife.

When you read the book of Hosea—and I do hope you will read through the whole book as well as following passages each day in these notes—you will find it a little confusing. The story of Hosea's marriage comes here, right at the beginning of the book, and then again in chapter three, and it is not simple nor obvious, even to some of the greatest biblical scholars, how we are supposed to link these texts to each other. Are there two marriages or is the same event described twice? Do not worry too much about this. Focus instead on the central, shocking image: the people of God have been unfaithful. They have worshipped other gods and have abandoned God's laws. They are behaving like a prostitute. To make the point plain, Hosea marries a prostitute himself. She bears him a son.

The marriage of Hosea to Gomer tells us three things that are then followed up throughout the rest of the book and are still very relevant for us today. First, God's enduring love, even for those who prostitute themselves and turn their back on God. Second, God's righteousness, and that there are consequences to our behaviour which bring terrible destruction and dis-ease. Third, God's longing to draw people back to himself.

Prayer

O God of love and judgement, draw us to yourself. Help us to see where we have turned away and lead us in the paths of peace.

STEPHEN COTTRELL

Dallying unfaithfulness

I will put an end to all her mirth, her festivals, her new moons, her sabbaths, and all her appointed festivals. I will lay waste her vines and her fig trees, of which she said, 'These are my pay, which my lovers have given me.' I will make them a forest, and the wild animals shall devour them. I will punish her for the festival days of the Baals, when she offered incense to them and decked herself with her ring and jewellery, and went after her lovers, and forgot me, says the Lord.

How easy it is to forget God—easy for the people of Israel, easy for us today. We do not want to seem different. A little compromise does not seem to matter. We will not forget God altogether, we say to ourselves, but, if we are not careful, babies are washed out with the bathwater.

When Israel forgets God and hankers after other ways, she is compared to a promiscuous woman, to be punished for going after other 'loves'. God looks contemptuously on the feasts and celebrations that honour these other gods—the Baals that Hosea speaks of. By its magisterial fidelity, God's love sits in judgement on our wretched infatuations and deceits. He threatens devastation to the land, showing us the inevitable consequences of our dallying unfaithfulness.

Although it is sometimes right to compromise and even though there is often good to be found in other ways, the danger is that one bit of forgetfulness can very easily lead to another. We must let God's commandments be our compass in life, showing us the right paths.

In the end, the people of Israel effectively stop following the God of the covenant made with Moses and become just like all the other people they live among. As God has chosen these people for a vocation that will, eventually in Christ, bring order and goodness to the whole world, this cannot continue. God has a purpose for them. They are the ones through whom he will become known to everyone. God has the same vocation for his church today—and we are part of that.

Prayer
O God of love and judgement, do not forget me.

STEPHEN COTTRELL

A door of hope

Therefore, I will now persuade her, and bring her into the wilderness, and speak tenderly to her. From there I will give her her vineyards, and make the Valley of Achor a door of hope.

With these verses the mood shifts. 'Therefore I will destroy…' becomes, 'Therefore I will persuade…' or, as another translation has it, 'I will allure'. Now God's language is the language of the lover, the one who speaks tenderly. We will look at this again later on, but, for today, let us concentrate on that enigmatic little phrase, 'I will make the Valley of Achor a door of hope'. What does this mean?

This is one of those bits of the Bible that does not make much sense unless you know some of the other bits as well. 'Achor' means 'bad luck' or 'despair' and the Valley of Achor is the place of shame, where one person's disobedience to God led to a devastating military defeat. In Joshua 7 you can read what happened and how great punishment was meted out to this person. The place where he and his family were stoned to death was called the Valley of Achor.

Here, however, Hosea is saying something astonishing. The place of disobedience and punishment will become the gateway to hope. It is an incredible redefining of how God will ultimately deal with waywardness and failure. It does not lead to destruction, but restitution. For Christians reading this passage, we are pointed straight to the cross, where we see the worst of sin but also the final nailing down of disobedience. It seems as if sin has triumphed, yet, similarly, the place of destruction, the cross, becomes the door of hope. God demonstrates the triumph of love and opens a door of hope at the centre of our most wilful failings, alluring us with the beautiful music of his love.

As we read these verses, therefore, we are reminded of the Christian truth that God meets us and delivers us at the point of our greatest failures. He does not punish us, but opens doors of hope via Jesus Christ.

Prayer

O God of love and judgement, in the failures and disappointments of my life open a door of hope.

Stephen Cottrell

Marriage renewed

On that day, says the Lord, you will call me, 'My husband', and no longer will you call me, 'My Baal'. For I will remove the names of the Baals from her mouth, and they shall be mentioned by name no more. I will make for you a covenant on that day with the wild animals, the birds of the air, and the creeping things of the ground; and I will abolish the bow, the sword, and war from the land; and I will make you lie down in safety. And I will take you for my wife for ever; I will take you for my wife in righteousness and in justice, in steadfast love, and in mercy. I will take you for my wife in faithfulness; and you shall know the Lord.

Hosea continues to tell us what it will be like when God's judgement brings restitution and peace and when we can at last know God face to face. It will be like a marriage. We will no longer hanker after other gods; not the Baals, who were the fertility gods of the other religions of Hosea's time, nor the idols of wealth and power that so easily seduce us today. Notice that God's covenant love, although focused on wayward but still dearly loved humanity, extends to the whole of the created order. Just as our disobedience affects the whole of creation, so does our restoration.

The image of a marriage between God and God's people describes a relationship of depth and endurance beyond what most people of that time thought their relationship with God was about. It is still challenging for us today. God loves us and is committed to us; he goes on loving us even when we fail. God's judgement is only concerned with what is best for the restoration of our relationship with him. This 'marriage' means that swords and bombs, chemical weapons and nuclear arms are abolished. They have no place in the kingdom of God. 'You will lie down in safety… I will take you for my wife in faithfulness,' says God, 'and you shall know the Lord.'

Prayer

O God of love and judgement, help us to know you and to enter into your covenant of peace.

STEPHEN COTTRELL

HOSEA 3:1–3 (NRSV)

Living it out

The Lord said to me again, 'Go, love a woman who has a lover and is an adulteress, just as the Lord loves the people of Israel, though they turn to other gods and love raisin cakes.' So I bought her for fifteen shekels of silver and a homer of barley and a measure of wine. And I said to her, 'You must remain as mine for many days; you shall not play the whore, you shall not have intercourse with a man, nor I with you.'

As we saw earlier, in order to learn the lesson of God's steadfast love, Hosea has been given the uncomfortable instruction to love and marry a prostitute. By doing this, he enters into the experience of unfaithfulness that so marked the behaviour of God's people and, in so doing, he also demonstrates the unflinching tenacity of God's love. Chapter 3 of the book returns to this story and this theme.

Although Hosea's living out of God's truth and judgement is an extreme version of what many prophets were asked to do, it is not necessarily so far away from some of the decisions and actions we have to make as disciples today. Every time we find ourselves having to choose to forgive when we do not feel very forgiving, or choose to be generous when we would rather keep things to ourselves, or stand up for justice when we would rather look the other way, we are living out a parable of God's goodness and judgement and love. We are embodying in our lives the truths and the values that we see in Christ. We are changed by it and so is the world.

Just as Hosea's ministry had a dramatic impact, so can our living out of the gospel. Others will be judged by our gracious behaviour and, at the same time, experience love. They may even be inspired to imitate such actions. Paul describes this in provocative language himself when he says, 'If your enemies are hungry, feed them; if they are thirsty, give them something to drink; for by doing this you will heap burning coals on their heads' (Romans 12:20).

Prayer

O God of love and judgement, help us to live out the values of the gospel.

STEPHEN COTTRELL

Creation suffering

Hear the word of the Lord, O people of Israel; for the Lord has an indictment against the inhabitants of the land. There is no faithfulness or loyalty, and no knowledge of God in the land. Swearing, lying, and murder, and stealing and adultery break out; bloodshed follows bloodshed. Therefore the land mourns, and all who live in it languish; together with the wild animals and the birds of the air, even the fish of the sea are perishing.

Hosea berates the people once again for their unfaithfulness and lists the many things they have done wrong. 'Bloodshed follows bloodshed', he says in a telling phrase, indicating how one bad thing gives birth to another. You cannot help but be reminded that, when Cain slew his brother Abel, God said to him, 'Your brother's blood is crying out to me from the ground!' (Genesis 4:10). In that passage the ground is cursed and in this passage we hear how the effect of Israel's unfaithfulness is that the very land is grieving. The animals, the birds, even the fish in the sea are all perishing. It is a terrible vision of the lifeblood of the world draining away.

In our own time, we can also see the intimate connection between our actions and the well-being of the earth. Our seas are overfished, our forests cut down, our air polluted, the balanced ecosystem endangered. If we stop to look, we can see around us today that the land is mourning.

As we shall see tomorrow, Hosea places the blame for Israel's unfaithful behaviour at the feet of the priests: the ones responsible for teaching and leading the people have themselves become the worst offenders. Now, we probably cannot blame climate change on the clergy of today, but it is important that all in leadership—especially those giving spiritual leadership—see the connection between our behaviour and the health of the earth itself. Part of our Christian responsibility is to be stewards of the earth. Hosea shows us what happens when we get this wrong.

Prayer

O God of love and judgement, help me to tread lightly on the earth and respect its fragile beauty.

Stephen Cottrell

Eaten up by greed

The more they increased, the more they sinned against me; they changed their glory into shame. They feed on the sin of my people; they are greedy for their iniquity. And it shall be like people, like priest; I will punish them for their ways, and repay them for their deeds. They shall eat, but not be satisfied; they shall play the whore, but not multiply; because they have forsaken the Lord to devote themselves to whoredom.

A failed and self-serving leadership has led to the downfall of Israel. The priests have forgotten God; the people have gone astray. The very things they turn to in their sinfulness fail to satisfy. Because they hunger for what they know to be wrong, they eat but are never full. The good things of the earth that God has given his people—food, companionship, sexual intimacy—are all exploited for selfish gain. The consequence is not pleasure, therefore, but pain and misery. It is a terrible and tragic image of where sin leads. You keep on eating but you are always hungry. Greed itself has eaten up your heart.

This sort of obsessive behaviour brings its own bitter reward. We probably know about it from first-hand experience, for few of us are completely addiction-free. Whether it is eating too much or spending too much time on the internet or much more dangerous addictions, such as alcohol or gambling, sexual promiscuity or pornography, they do not satisfy but only lead to greater and more self-destructive cravings.

Further on in this chapter—again making reference to the worship of other gods—Hosea says that 'my people consult a piece of wood' (v. 12). This is the root of the problem. People have abandoned the goodness and guiding principles of God. It is not enough to follow your conscience if your conscience is not being formed and, where necessary, rebuked by the guidance of a God who alone knows what is good and true and helpful for prosperous living.

Prayer

O God of love and judgement, help me to set my compass by the strength and goodness of your word and set me free from the hunger of my addictions.

STEPHEN COTTRELL

Showers of blessing

'Come, let us return to the Lord; for it is he who has torn, and he will heal us; he has struck down, and he will bind us up. After two days he will revive us; on the third day he will raise us up, that we may live before him. Let us know, let us press on to know the Lord; his appearing is as sure as the dawn; he will come to us like the showers, like the spring rains that water the earth.'

Chapters 4 and 5 of Hosea heap condemnation on God's people for their faithless behaviour. The priests are told that the 'spirit of whore-dom is within them' (5:4). Everything seems dark and hopeless. Then suddenly in chapter 6 we find this beautiful call to repentance. Hosea cries out that the same God who has torn us will heal us and the one who has struck us down will bind us up. These words feel like a dazzling burst of sunlight breaking into a darkened room or a refreshing shower of rain on barren ground, which is precisely how Hosea describes it: God's appearing will be like the dawn and 'the spring rains that water the earth' (v. 3).

Even within this appeal to 'return to the Lord', Hosea stresses, there must also be an acknowledgement that all that has happened came from God in the first place. The people are asking God to deliver them from a misery that is the consequence of their own wilful faithlessness. This God of justice, however, is also a God of mercy. It is this revelation of God's character that the book of Hosea lays before us. The one who strikes down will also lift up.

Of course, it is impossible for Christians to read this passage without also thinking of another who was struck down—not because of his faithlessness, but because of his astonishing obedience—and was also vindicated by God and raised on the third day.

Prayer

O God of love and judgement, help us to acknowledge our failings, seek your truth and receive the refreshing blessings of your peace.

STEPHEN COTTRELL

Love, not sacrifice

What shall I do with you, O Ephraim? What shall I do with you, O Judah? Your love is like a morning cloud, like the dew that goes away early. Therefore I have hewn them by the prophets, I have killed them by the words of my mouth, and my judgement goes forth as the light. For I desire steadfast love and not sacrifice, the knowledge of God rather than burnt-offerings.

God's love is as sure as the dawn; our love, says God, is like the morning mist, quickly disappearing. 'What shall I do with you?' says God (v. 4). As we go deeper into the book of Hosea, we shall see that God's answer to this question is to go on loving, giving us that self-emptying and tenacious love shown to us in the life of Christ.

Here, Hosea speaks of God's judgement as light—an image taken up in John's Gospel, where Jesus himself says, 'This is the judgement, that the light has come into the world, and people loved darkness rather than light because their deeds were evil' (3:19).

The light of God's judgement shows us how things really are, including our own motives and behaviour. What God desires—and this is another of the great steps forward that we find in Hosea—is not just good behaviour and pure motives but also steadfast love. The love, which makes God's judgement restorative and purifying, means that we are called to serve and know God by love. Not only should we refrain from offering sacrifices to other gods; the one true God does not want sacrifices either, except the sacrifice of a humble, loving and obedient heart. It is knowledge of this God of love and judgement that will save us, not a burnt offering.

Such a demonstration of love leads to only one place: the cross of Christ. The psalmist says, 'Steadfast love and faithfulness will meet' and 'righteousness and peace will kiss each other' (Psalm 85:10). On the cross, perfect love is laid out in painful detail. It is the place where we can bring our failings and make the offering of our hearts.

Prayer

O God of love and judgement, shine your light on me and lead me to the cross of Christ.

STEPHEN COTTRELL

Reaping the whirlwind

For they sow the wind, and they shall reap the whirlwind. The standing grain has no heads, it shall yield no meal; if it were to yield, foreigners would devour it. Israel is swallowed up; now they are among the nations as a useless vessel.

Hosea returns to the theme of judgement and Israel's apostasy. He uses a powerful image of what happens when you lose your bearings and do things the wrong way round: you sow a wind and reap a whirlwind. In other words, a relatively small wrong action returns as a crashing and destructive tempest. He follows this up with another potent image of the wheat standing in the fields: it looks as if the harvest is ready, but there is no grain. Even if there were, others would eat it, and the sowers would get nothing.

As this chapter continues, Hosea speaks again of Ephraim's whoring after other gods, Israel's exile and the people's disregard for God's statutes. God will remember their iniquity, he says, 'and punish their sins; they shall return to Egypt' (v. 13). It is like the exodus in reverse: Israel is banished from the promised land and returned to slavery.

It is hard to imagine what such a backwards journey might feel like, but such warnings are still relevant to us today. Even small wrongdoings and selfish actions can reap devastating consequences in our lives and the lives of others. We will be like wheat that looks good, but has nothing to offer. As Jesus puts it in Luke's Gospel (6:43–46):

'No good tree bears bad fruit, nor again does a bad tree bear good fruit; for each tree is known by its own fruit. Figs are not gathered from thorns, nor are grapes picked from a bramble bush. The good person out of the good treasure of the heart produces good, and the evil person out of evil treasure produces evil; for it is out of the abundance of the heart that the mouth speaks. Why do you call me "Lord, Lord", and do not do what I tell you?'

Prayer

O God of love and judgement, help me to sow good things, that I may reap a harvest of righteousness.

STEPHEN COTTRELL

17

The importance of roots

Sow for yourselves righteousness; reap steadfast love; break up your fallow ground; for it is time to seek the Lord, that he may come and rain righteousness upon you. You have ploughed wickedness, you have reaped injustice, you have eaten the fruit of lies.

Chapters 9 and 10 of Hosea use again the image of sowing and reaping that we explored yesterday. This time it is even clearer that righteousness must be sown, for this will bring the spring showers of God's righteousness. Moreover, the good tree, if it is to produce good fruit, must be planted in good soil and close to refreshing waters. In fact, that great book of biblical wisdom, the Psalms, opens with this image (Psalm 1).

In chapter 9, God says through Hosea that he first found Israel 'like grapes in the wilderness... like the first fruit on the fig tree, in its first season' (v. 10). In other words, God remembers the good beginnings for Israel. Note how, in Hosea, God often calls his people 'Ephraim'. Ephraim, you may remember, was Joseph's second son, born to him while in exile in Egypt and dearly loved. Using that name suggests a certain tenderness, which will be brought out even more in tomorrow's passage.

For now, we are invited to remember that God knows his people were planted in a good place and destined to bear good fruit, but they worshipped other gods and prostituted themselves. By doing this, they almost literally uprooted themselves: 'Ephraim is stricken,' says God, 'their root is dried up, they shall bear no fruit' (v. 16). This is even more poignant when we remember that the name 'Ephraim' means 'fruitful'.

Reading this as Christians, we remember that we, too, need to be planted and rooted in a place that will nourish and refresh us—which is in Christ. As Jesus says, 'Those who abide in me and I in them bear much fruit, because apart from me you can do nothing' (John 15:5).

Prayer

O God of love and judgement, help me to make my home in Christ; shower your righteousness on me.

Stephen Cottrell

My child Ephraim

When Israel was a child, I loved him, and out of Egypt I called my son. The more I called them, the more they went from me... Yet it was I who taught Ephraim to walk, I took them up in my arms; but they did not know that I healed them. I led them with cords of human kindness, with bands of love. I was to them like those who lift infants to their cheeks. I bent down to them and fed them.

This is one of the most amazing passages in the whole of the Old Testament. With very little precedent, we are offered this remarkable image of God as the loving father, reaching out to his wayward children. 'It was I who taught them to walk': this is such a beautiful image, for what parents do not remember the first faltering steps of their children? What we see here is not God's judgement so much as God's terrible sadness.

Note that, again, God calls his people 'Ephraim'—the name of one of the main tribes of Israel. Joshua was from this tribe, which was part of the northern kingdom of Israel and was to fall at the time of the Assyrian conquest.

We see here the dawning understanding of God's true character, the Father God Jesus teaches us about. God is like a loving parent; one who loves us with the same self-giving love with which we love our children. God delights in us. God weeps over our failures and will try and try again to show us what is good. His judgement and his love cannot be separated.

Hosea finally announces that 'Assyria will be their king' (11:5)—Israel goes into exile. God also declares his unyielding faithfulness: 'How can I give you up, Ephraim?... My heart recoils within me; my compassion grows warm and tender. I will not execute my fierce anger... for I am God and no mortal, the Holy One in your midst, and I will not come in wrath' (11:8–9).

Prayer
O God of love and judgement, be my Father and I your beloved child. Teach me your ways and show me your compassion.

STEPHEN COTTRELL

In God's shadow

Return, O Israel, to the Lord your God, for you have stumbled because of your iniquity… I will love them freely, for my anger has turned from them. I will be like the dew to Israel; he shall blossom like the lily… His shoots shall spread out; his beauty shall be like the olive tree, and his fragrance like that of Lebanon. They shall again live beneath my shadow, they shall flourish as a garden; they shall blossom like the vine… O Ephraim, what have I to do with idols? It is I who answer and look after you. I am like an evergreen cypress; your faithfulness comes from me… For the ways of the Lord are right, and the upright walk in them, but transgressors stumble in them.

Hosea ends with God again calling Israel to repentance, promising to heal their waywardness and love them freely. Then there will be great blessing. Some of the Bible's greatest images are found in this final chapter: God will bless his people like morning dew, they shall blossom like the lily and the vine, they shall be fruitful and fragrant (vv. 5–7). This has particular poignancy, since Israel had lusted after the fertility gods of other religions. 'I am like an evergreen cypress,' says God (v. 8), always fruitful.

We also find here the mysterious image of God's shadow: 'They shall again live beneath my shadow; they shall flourish as a garden; they shall blossom like the vine' (v. 7). The psalms often speak of protection being found under the shadow of God's protecting wing (see, for example, Psalms 17:8 and 91:1). Also, when telling Mary she is to be the mother of the Lord, the angel Gabriel says that the power of the Most High will 'overshadow' her (Luke 1:35) and, in Acts (5:14–16), Peter's passing shadow brings healing and blessing.

So, we can heed Hosea's warning, but we can also delight in his promises. Let us return to the Lord, abide in Christ our true vine and dwell beneath the shadow of God's presence.

Prayer

O God of love and judgement, help me to live faithfully under the shadow of your protection, and may my life be fruitful.

STEPHEN COTTRELL

2 Kings 22—25

Reading the stories of 2 Kings is rather like reading W.C. Sellar and R.J. Yeatman's classic parody of British history *1066 and All That* (Methuen, 2010), with its alternations of Good Kings, Bad Kings, Good Things and Bad Things. None of the rulers described seems to be a mix of good and bad; the book's judgements on them are swift and decisive.

How reliable is the narrator or narrators in their assessment of the rulers described? We cannot know, but we can note that the kings are judged not on their political effectiveness, management of the nation's economy, success in war against other nations or ability to fend off potential invaders. No, they are classified according to whether or not they 'did what was right in the sight of the Lord' or 'did what was evil in the sight of the Lord'. This is determined largely by their religious observance—whether they worship God alone in the temple at Jerusalem or turn to the gods of the local pagans and set up shrines to them around the country. The implication, however, is that worship of pagan gods will lead to injustice, exploitation and oppression, while worship of God will lead to justice and neighbourly love. So, it is not just about how worship is practised.

There are precious few kings who 'did what was right', but the consequences of righteousness and wickedness are clear. Above all, the reign of Josiah shows the role of God's revelation in promoting righteousness, as 'the Book of the Law' is found during temple repairs.

What can 21st-century people learn from these ancient documents, describing a time and place with customs and political institutions so different from ours? Well, while culture has changed, people still have the same motivations: power, the desire for admiration, wanting to influence events. Whatever roles of authority we have in life—as a manager, a church leader, a parent—the kings of Judah paint for us a picture of what it means to govern well or govern badly. At the heart of governing well is God's communication with us—for Judah, in the Bible and for us supremely in Jesus.

Veronica Zundel

2 KINGS 22:1–7 (NRSV, ABRIDGED)

Honesty breeds honesty

Josiah was eight years old when he began to reign; he reigned for thirty-one years in Jerusalem. His mother's name was Jedidah daughter of Adaiah of Bozkath. He did what was right in the sight of the Lord, and walked in all the way of his father David; he did not turn aside to the right or to the left. In the eighteenth year of King Josiah, the king sent Shaphan... the secretary, to the house of the Lord, saying, 'Go up to the high priest Hilkiah, and have him count the entire sum of the money that has been brought into the house of the Lord... let it be given into the hand of the workers who have the oversight of the house of the Lord; let them give it to the workers who are at the house of the Lord, repairing the house... to buy timber and quarried stone to repair the house. But no account shall be asked from them for the money that is delivered into their hand, for they deal honestly.'

In the town hall of the Italian city of Siena, there are two murals depicting the same town. In one, all is ordered and calm: workmen are repairing buildings; citizens are going about their business; a throned figure of Wisdom holds the scales of Justice. In the other, chaos rules: a horned figure of Tyranny dominates the scene; Justice lies bound on the ground.

These murals recall 1 and 2 Kings, with their evil and righteous kings. Josiah is one of the few righteous ones, but what is most remarkable is that he is the son and grandson of kings who 'did evil'. Where did he learn the service of God—and at such a young age? Perhaps it was from his mother Jedidah, as Jesus no doubt learned at the feet of Mary, the prophet of the Magnificat.

More remarkably still, Josiah creates a culture of honesty in his kingdom, so that he can trust his workers from the top tier (the secretary) to the bottom (those working on the temple). What political leaders can you think of who have set such a good example?

Prayer

Pray for justice and honesty in government, in your own country and elsewhere.

VERONICA ZUNDEL

2 KINGS 22:8, 10–13 (NRSV)

Book of life

The high priest Hilkiah said to Shaphan the secretary, 'I have found the book of the law in the house of the Lord.'… Shaphan the secretary informed the king, 'The priest Hilkiah has given me a book.' Shaphan then read it aloud to the king. When the king heard the words of the book of the law, he tore his clothes. Then the king commanded the priest Hilkiah, Ahikam son of Shaphan, Achbor son of Micaiah, Shaphan the secretary, and the king's servant Asaiah, saying, 'Go, inquire of the Lord for me, for the people, and for all Judah, concerning the words of this book that has been found; for great is the wrath of the Lord that is kindled against us, because our ancestors did not obey the words of this book.'

The Christian songwriter Garth Hewitt recently set to music a number of hymns from the hymn book of the 19th-century Chartist movement for democracy. They had three different hymn books, but only a single copy of one survives. Imagine for a moment if there were no more Bibles in the world. How would you feel if you came across a surviving copy, even if it was incomplete?

The Hebrew Bible (Old Testament) as we know it was not written down at this point: its stories were conveyed by an oral tradition. Oral transmission can be quite accurate because people without books have well-trained memories, but, of course, details and sometimes whole chunks can be lost.

We might think that Josiah would be thrilled to have this copy of what was probably part of Deuteronomy, yet he is appalled. He uses the gestures of bereavement to express his distress for the evil that has come about because previous kings and their people did not obey this book.

He does not rely on his own perception of the situation, however. He wants to call in an 'expert', a prophet of God, to explain how he must act. When we have difficult situations or decisions facing us, a second opinion from a person we respect is always welcome.

Prayer

Thank God for not only the Bible but also all books that inspire us in faith and life.

VERONICA ZUNDEL

A woman's word

So the priest Hilkiah, Ahikam, Achbor, Shaphan, and Asaiah went to the prophetess Huldah the wife of Shallum son of Tikvah, son of Harhas, keeper of the wardrobe… She declared to them, 'Thus says the Lord, the God of Israel: Tell the man who sent you to me… I will indeed bring disaster on this place and on its inhabitants… But as to the king of Judah, who sent you to inquire of the Lord, thus shall you say to him… Regarding the words that you have heard, because your heart was penitent, and you humbled yourself before the Lord… and because you have torn your clothes and wept before me, I also have heard you, says the Lord. Therefore, I will gather you to your ancestors, and you shall be gathered to your grave in peace; your eyes shall not see all the disaster that I will bring on this place.'

I was shocked when I found that my husband, who was brought up to 'know the Bible backwards', had not heard of Huldah. Clearly he did not know it forwards! Mind you, I only discovered her a few years ago myself. How has this woman prophet—arguably the first biblical interpreter—been so forgotten? Could it be that we approach the Bible assuming there were no female prophets, so we simply do not see her? In a world where a woman's testimony was not legally valid, God called her to speak the word. She is crucial to the Bible's history.

Notice that she does not give a detailed exposition of the book Hilkiah found. Instead, she goes straight to its relevance for God's people, which is that, because they have neglected and disobeyed its commandments, their society will face disaster (although Josiah himself will be spared).

It is important for us to delve into the Bible's linguistic and cultural background and its meaning for those who first heard or read it. However, all this is useless unless we can see what difference it makes to how we live. We must also not get so bogged down in detail that we miss the broad themes of scripture—justice, peace, love of God and neighbour.

Reflection
Are we failing to recognise prophetic women today?

VERONICA ZUNDEL

All in it together

Then the king directed that all the elders of Judah and Jerusalem should be gathered to him. The king went up to the house of the Lord, and with him went all the people of Judah, all the inhabitants of Jerusalem, the priests, the prophets, and all the people, both small and great; he read in their hearing all the words of the book of the covenant that had been found in the house of the Lord. The king stood by the pillar and made a covenant before the Lord, to follow the Lord, keeping his commandments, his decrees, and his statutes, with all his heart and all his soul, to perform the words of this covenant that were written in this book. All the people joined in the covenant.

In my church, we practise consensus decision-making. We do not move forward until all of us at least consent to an action, even if we do not agree with it 100 per cent. It is slow, but, at its best, it ensures that we avoid church splits or arbitrarily imposed decisions.

Josiah did not see obedience to God as a matter that could be decided by the king alone; he wanted everyone in the kingdom to be on board. That meant everyone needed to know as much about God's ways as he did, so the first thing he did was to read the book to everyone. If Judah was to follow the covenant he made, they had to understand what the covenant entailed.

We often think of salvation as an individual matter, based on an individual decision, but the Bible's view of salvation (or redemption) is much broader: it encompasses the whole of society and every aspect of human life. We do not have a theocracy (a God-ruled society) as the Israelites had and, in fact, they had already moved away from this by appointing a king (1 Samuel 8:4–7). We cannot declare 'Everyone in this country is a Christian', which was patently never true. What we can do, however, is to recognise that following Jesus is a communal matter: we cannot do it alone; it is too hard.

Reflection

What does your church do to ensure that its members will disciple each other?

VERONICA ZUNDEL

Root and branch

The king commanded the high priest Hilkiah, the priests of the second order, and the guardians of the threshold, to bring out of the temple of the Lord all the vessels made for Baal, for Asherah, and for all the host of heaven… He deposed the idolatrous priests whom the kings of Judah had ordained to make offerings in the high places at the cities of Judah and around Jerusalem… He brought out the image of Asherah from the house of the Lord… burned it at the Wadi Kidron, beat it to dust and threw the dust of it upon the graves of the common people. He broke down the houses of the male temple prostitutes that were in the house of the Lord… He defiled Topheth, which is in the valley of Ben-hinnom, so that no one would make a son or a daughter pass through fire as an offering to Molech.

As an example of interfaith dialogue, this does not stand up very well! Look closely at the kind of 'religion' Josiah was outlawing, though— male temple prostitutes, child sacrifice. This is a long way from ideas of working together with all people of good will. What he hated was essentially abusive religion bound up with sexual exploitation, violence and amorality. For the people of God to live as God wanted them to, it had to be destroyed, root and branch.

We can be uncomfortable with some parts of the Old Testament's insistence on the destruction of idolatry. Maybe it becomes more understandable if we look at some of today's idolatries, which are less obvious (we do not generally set up images of gods), but equally destructive. What about the idolatry of consumerism that keeps half the planet poor and damages the environment? The idolatry of a 'right to sex' that creates a view of women as mere commodities? The idolatry of 'security' that involves keeping enough weapons to destroy the world several times over?

When we seek to drive out evil, however, we need to be quite sure we know what we are replacing it with—as Josiah did.

Prayer
Lord Jesus, teach us how to drive out evil with good, not more evil.

VERONICA ZUNDEL

Celebrate life

The king commanded all the people, 'Keep the passover to the Lord your God as prescribed in this book of the covenant.' No such passover had been kept since the days of the judges... even during all the days of the kings of Israel and of the kings of Judah; but in the eighteenth year of King Josiah this passover was kept to the Lord in Jerusalem... Before him there was no king like him, who turned to the Lord with all his heart, with all his soul, and with all his might, according to all the law of Moses; nor did any like him arise after him. Still the Lord did not turn from the fierceness of his great wrath, by which his anger was kindled against Judah, because of all the provocations with which Manasseh had provoked him. The Lord said, 'I will remove Judah also out of my sight, as I have removed Israel; and I will reject this city that I have chosen, Jerusalem.'

Apparently 'Sunday Assembly'— a regular gathering for atheists—has spread to 20 cities around the world! People need a way to mark shared commitments, even a commitment to *not* believing.

Josiah was not going to drive out idols from the house of God but then leave it empty (Luke 11:24–26). His positive action was to reintroduce the worship of God—and not just some general act of worship, but the one that best commemorated God's liberation of the people. Worship is to be based in real memories of God acting in history.

Is our worship sometimes too general? Do we need to introduce into it ways to celebrate how God has acted, not just for individuals within the congregation but also the whole congregation, our country, our world? Could we celebrate in our worship, for instance, the fact that, over the last few decades, violence worldwide has significantly reduced? Do not believe all you hear—good news is rarely reported, but it exists.

Reflection

God still apparently rejects Judah in this passage. Yet, centuries later, Jesus would come to Judah and Paul would ask, 'Has God rejected his people? By no means!' (Romans 11:1).

Veronica Zundel

Death and taxes

Jehoahaz was twenty-three years old when he began to reign; he reigned for three months in Jerusalem. His mother's name was Hamutal daughter of Jeremiah of Libnah. He did what was evil in the sight of the Lord, just as his ancestors had done. Pharaoh Neco confined him at Riblah in the land of Hamath... and imposed tribute on the land of one hundred talents of silver and a talent of gold. Pharaoh Neco made Eliakim son of Josiah king in place of his father Josiah, and changed his name to Jehoiakim. But he took Jehoahaz away; he came to Egypt, and died there. Jehoiakim gave the silver and the gold to Pharaoh, but he taxed the land in order to meet Pharaoh's demand for money. He exacted the silver and the gold from the people of the land, from all according to their assessment.

Have you ever noticed how children can reflect characteristics of their grandparents more than those of their parents? Similarly, Jehoahaz had little in common with his father Josiah, but more with his grandfather and great-grandfather, who 'did what was evil in the sight of the Lord' (v. 32). As a younger brother he should not have been king: perhaps the people preferred him or he was imposed on them by the local super-power, Egypt. Whatever the situation, he failed to pay the tribute demanded by them. Was this an attempt to assert his independence and the reason Pharaoh imprisoned and then deported him?

His older brother was not much more than a puppet king, unable even to choose his own 'throne name'. He paid the tribute, but passed on the cost to his people. He does not seem to have been an unjust king as he assessed the people's means and taxed them accordingly—what today we might call 'progressive taxation'. Tax is a good thing when it compels individuals to contribute to the common good, but, in this case, it only served to placate an ancient enemy. I often think the Bible would make a very interesting commentary on relations between small and more powerful countries today.

Reflection

Do you think taxation is fair in your country? Is the tax well spent?

VERONICA ZUNDEL

Political two-timing

In his days King Nebuchadnezzar of Babylon came up; Jehoiakim became his servant for three years; then he turned and rebelled against him. The Lord sent against him bands of the Chaldeans, bands of the Arameans, bands of the Moabites, and bands of the Ammonites; he sent them against Judah to destroy it, according to the word of the Lord that he spoke by his servants the prophets. Surely this came upon Judah at the command of the Lord, to remove them out of his sight, for the sins of Manasseh… and also for the innocent blood that he had shed, So Jehoiakim slept with his ancestors; then his son Jehoiachin succeeded him. The king of Egypt did not come again out of his land, for the king of Babylon had taken over all that belonged to the king of Egypt from the Wadi of Egypt to the River Euphrates.

Many people these days have two jobs, but it can be hard to stop the demands of one encroaching on the other. Jesus famously said that 'No one can serve two masters' (Matthew 6:24), though he was talking of God and wealth, of course. Jehoiakim seems to have tried to disprove this because, as well as paying tribute to Egypt, he becomes a 'vassal king' of Babylon. Or could he just see which way the wind was blowing? We learn in verse 7 that Babylon was taking over the superpower status of Egypt. Empires rise and fall and there is always a new one to take over when the old one loses power.

Soon, Jehoiakim attempts to go it alone. The writer attributes his subsequent defeat to the hand of God, as punishment for the sins and violence of his ancestor Manasseh. Many Old Testament writers believed that the sins of the parents would be visited on their children (Exodus 34:7). However, the prophets said that, in future times, only the person who sins will be punished (Jeremiah 31:29–30; Ezekiel 18:2–4). We can see a progression here that will culminate in the forgiveness of our sins through Jesus.

Prayer

Lord, when I am tempted to serve another master, show me that it is impossible and lead me back to full commitment.

VERONICA ZUNDEL

The end is not the end

Jehoiachin... reigned for three months in Jerusalem... He did what was evil in the sight of the Lord, just as his father had done. At that time the servants of King Nebuchadnezzar of Babylon came up to Jerusalem, and the city was besieged... King Jehoiachin of Judah gave himself up to the king of Babylon, himself, his mother, his servants, his officers, and his palace officials. The king of Babylon... carried off all the treasures of the house of the Lord, and the treasures of the king's house... He carried away all Jerusalem, all the officials, all the warriors, ten thousand captives, all the artisans and the smiths; no one remained, except the poorest people of the land. He carried away Jehoiachin to Babylon; the king's mother, the king's wives, his officials, and the elite of the land, he took into captivity from Jerusalem to Babylon... [He] made Mattaniah, Jehoiachin's uncle, king in his place and changed his name to Zedekiah.

If you have had a great tragedy in your life, you will never forget it. This conquest, second only to their slavery in Egypt, was the great tragedy of the Jewish people (until the 20th century, that is). Though they would eventually return, their hold on the promised land was never the same and they remembered the exile in Babylon as modern-day Jews remember the Holocaust. No one was unaffected and subsequent generations would look back to it as if they themselves had been there when it happened, just as the Passover liturgy asks us to see the exodus as if we ourselves were freed from Egypt.

Yet, the Babylonian exile was in some ways the making of the people of God. In Babylon, they first forged a distinctive identity in a foreign land. Central to this was their gathering of the documents and oral traditions that would make up the Jewish scriptures and later became the basis of our Christian scriptures. Never forget that three-quarters of the Bible was not written by Christians!

Suffering and drastic change have a way of concentrating the mind on what is most important. Has this been true for you?

Reflection

When things go wrong, we learn who our best friends are—not least, God.

Veronica Zundel

Rebel without a cause?

Zedekiah rebelled against the king of Babylon. And in the ninth year of his reign... King Nebuchadnezzar of Babylon came with all his army against Jerusalem, and laid siege to it... So the city was besieged until the eleventh year of King Zedekiah. On the ninth day of the fourth month the famine became so severe in the city that there was no food for the people of the land. Then a breach was made in the city wall; the king with all the soldiers fled by night by the way of the gate between the two walls, by the king's garden... But the army of the Chaldeans pursued the king, and overtook him in the plains of Jericho; all his army was scattered, deserting him. Then they captured the king and brought him up to the king of Babylon at Riblah, who passed sentence on him. They slaughtered the sons of Zedekiah before his eyes, then put out the eyes of Zedekiah; they bound him in fetters and took him to Babylon.

I read a piece on the internet about the various alliances between different governments and political groups in the Middle East. It was so complex that I gave up trying to work it out!

International alliances in the ancient Middle East were not quite so complicated, but kings (who were the only form of government around) often switched alliances and caused regional conflict. Zedekiah is as fickle in his allegiance as Jehoiakim before him. By rebelling, he is biting the hand that feeds him, for it was Babylon who appointed him king in his nephew's place. His attempt to gain more power for himself results in war, famine and general disaster for the people and, eventually, leads to the complete conquest of Judah. Unwise government affects more than just those who govern.

We who have democracy, however flawed it can be, at least have the chance to change our government periodically. Ill-advised foreign policy, however, can still lead to suffering for many. What can we do to call our government to account for its decisions?

Prayer

Pray for good government in countries that lack it—and in your own.

VERONICA ZUNDEL

Reduced to ruins

In the fifth month, on the seventh day of the month... Nebuzaradan, the captain of the bodyguard... came to Jerusalem. He burned the house of the Lord, the king's house, and all the houses of Jerusalem; every great house he burned down. All the army of the Chaldeans who were with the captain of the guard broke down the walls around Jerusalem. Nebuzaradan the captain of the guard carried into exile the rest of the people who were left in the city and the deserters who had defected to the king of Babylon—all the rest of the population. But the captain of the guard left some of the poorest people of the land to be vine-dressers and tillers of the soil... So Judah went into exile out of its land.

There can be something very romantic about ruins. We can let our imagination roam around them, picturing the fascinating lives people once led there. Some great landowners even built fake ruins—'follies'— to make their grounds more attractive. This, though, is a rose-coloured view: in reality so many ruins tell stories of war, plunder and destruction or simply financial catastrophe.

The Babylonians are determined to destroy every trace of Jewish residence in Judah, leaving only a few people to care for the land that is now theirs. Part of this, perhaps, is the occupying power's desire to put its own stamp on its conquest; part of it may be an outlet for the aggression of armies that have been trained to destroy.

Contrast this with the promises of God given by Isaiah (61:4–5): 'They shall build up the ancient ruins, they shall raise up the former devastations; they shall repair the ruined cities, the devastations of many generations. Strangers shall stand and feed your flocks, foreigners shall till your land and dress your vines.' Ruins may be romantic, but restored houses are what people need to live in! The Bible may sometimes see God as the punisher of evil, but it overwhelmingly sees God as the restorer of good.

Prayer

Think of a country where there are currently a lot of ruins, through war or poverty, and pray for restoration.

Veronica Zundel

Naming the loss

The bronze pillars that were in the house of the Lord, as well as the stands and the bronze sea that were in the house of the Lord, the Chaldeans broke in pieces, and carried the bronze to Babylon. They took away the pots, the shovels, the snuffers, the dishes for incense, and all the bronze vessels used in the temple service, as well as the firepans and the basins. What was made of gold the captain of the guard took away for the gold, and what was made of silver, for the silver. As for the two pillars, the one sea, and the stands, which Solomon had made for the house of the Lord the bronze of all these vessels was beyond weighing.

In a burglary some years ago, I lost an elaborate, highly engraved gold bracelet that came from my late grandmother. What saddened me most was that this beautiful artefact, which had survived since about the 1920s or 1930s, would probably be melted down for just the value of the weight of the gold that had been used to make it. Similarly, how painful it must have been for the people of God to see the objects that enhanced their worship treated as nothing more than a source of precious metals for financial gain. Worse, they may have been reshaped into idols of the non-existent gods the Babylonians worshipped and, thus, become unholy rather than holy things.

Often the special objects within a beloved, and now lost, place can be as much missed as the place itself. The pillars, stands, sacred objects, curtains and vessels of the temple were visible, tangible reminders for the Judeans of what this holy place meant to them. These things had been made with love and reverence by talented craftspeople and accumulated their own history through their use. They would not be easy to replace.

What most symbolises the worship and service of God for us today? Is it sacred objects or particular liturgies or the building we worship in? If we have lost them, how can we name in our worship what they stood for? Mourning can be as important in our times together as rejoicing, as the many psalms of lament in the Bible show.

Reflection
Precious objects are replaceable; people, who make them, are not.

VERONICA ZUNDEL

The law in their own hands

[The king] appointed Gedaliah... as governor over the people who remained in the land of Judah... Now when all the captains of the forces and their men heard that the king of Babylon had appointed Gedaliah as governor, they came with their men to Gedaliah at Mizpah... Gedaliah swore to them and their men, saying, 'Do not be afraid because of the Chaldean officials; live in the land, serve the king of Babylon, and it shall be well with you.' But in the seventh month, Ishmael son of Nethaniah son of Elishama, of the royal family, came with ten men; they struck down Gedaliah so that he died, along with the Judeans and Chaldeans who were with him at Mizpah. Then all the people, high and low, and the captains of the forces, set out and went to Egypt; for they were afraid of the Chaldeans.

A late member of my church used to say it was better to have a government, however bad, than to have none, resulting in chaos. Those left in Judah needed the rule of law, even if it was imposed by Nebuchadnezzar. Gedaliah sounds reassuring enough, but he was ultimately a foreign ruler, imposed by an occupying power—hence the plot to assassinate him (political coups are nothing new!).

It is one thing to take the law into your own hands; it is another to face the consequences. As soon as they realise the implications of what they have done, not only the assassins but also all the people flee—predictably, to the previous local superpower. Punishment from Babylon for the killing of their representative would have been swift and merciless.

All around the world, unjust or unpopular governments are overthrown by violence, but the regime that follows is seldom much better than the last. If you use violence to gain power, you may also use it to maintain power; violence begets more violence. There are also, however, individuals and groups around the world seeking to learn 'the things that make for peace' (Luke 19:42): non-violent ways of resistance, techniques of conflict resolution. We need to learn from them.

Pray

Pray for any organisations you know of that work for peace in situations of conflict.

VERONICA ZUNDEL

Goodness in Babylon

In the thirty-seventh year of the exile of King Jehoiachin of Judah, in the twelfth month, on the twenty-seventh day of the month, King Evil-merodach of Babylon, in the year that he began to reign, released King Jehoiachin of Judah from prison; he spoke kindly to him, and gave him a seat above the other seats of the kings who were with him in Babylon. So Jehoiachin put aside his prison clothes. Every day of his life he dined regularly in the king's presence. For his allowance, a regular allowance was given him by the king, a portion every day, as long as he lived.

'Babylon' has been a code word for the powers of injustice ever since the Bible was written: its meaning can be seen even in the songs of reggae star Bob Marley. Yet here we find a king, the son and successor of Nebuchadnezzar, who, despite his name's unfortunate sound in English, acts compassionately to the captive former king of Judah who has been deposed by Babylon.

Is this just a case of kings sticking together, or of one rogue recognising another and being 'thick as thieves'? (Jehoiachin was, after all, a king 'who did evil in the sight of the Lord'.) I hope not. Daniel 4:28–36 recounts the apparent mental illness and turning to God of Nebuchadnezzar. Could some of this have rubbed off on his son?

Whatever the truth, Evil-Merodach acts magnanimously, which speaks well of him. Even in the midst of an 'evil empire' (and there are plenty of them in history), we can find goodness and generosity. It is never a simple case of 'the good guys' versus 'the bad guys' in international relations. All of us are capable of great evil and great good, according to our circumstances, character and, most of all, the commitments we make.

So, as we come to the end of the stories of 'good kings' and 'bad kings', we realise that no ruler, or subject, is ever totally good or bad. We all need to be redeemed and transformed by God's love.

Reflection

God is the only purely good king. What does it mean to you to 'dine regularly at the king's table'? What 'regular allowance' would you like from God?

VERONICA ZUNDEL

My favourite scriptures

This series of 14 readings comes under the title 'My favourite scriptures'. I confess, at first it was a title I found difficult. What is the point in having 'favourite' scriptures? Is that not just picking the bits we like and avoiding the awkward passages? Yet…

One of the things that becomes apparent after reading the scriptures over many years is, however much we treasure the Bible as a whole, some parts seem to speak to us more than others. As the poet Samuel Taylor Coleridge argued in his little book *Confessions of an Inquiring Spirit*, we do the Bible no favours if we 'flatten' the text and expect every sentence to speak with exactly the same depth. Like any book, the literary gems have to be held within interlocking texts, such that the whole hangs together. But there are some parts that sparkle for us more than others, and some parts seem prosaic while others speak volumes. Of course, which is which may differ from one person to the next.

'In the Bible,' Coleridge wrote, 'there is more that finds me than I have experienced in all other books put together… the words of the Bible find me at greater depths of my being; and… whatever finds me brings with it an irresistible evidence of its having proceeded from the Holy Spirit.'

Matthew Arnold later called this statement Coleridge's 'happy phrase about the Bible', and it gives the sense that describing one's 'favourite' scriptures is not merely an exercise in cherry picking or choosing what is palatable and leaving what is challenging. Rather, it is about identifying those passages that, repeatedly over time, have 'spoken' to us—to challenge, comfort or promise—and evoked a response that takes us beyond ourselves.

It is in this spirit that I share 14 passages that I have chosen from the pages of the Bible. They have appealed to me at different moments, with my particular concerns as a songwriter, theologian and a woman in a man's world. Some will be very familiar, some a little more obscure, but all of them have 'found me'.

Maggi Dawn

Do not settle for less

Terah was the father of Abram, Nahor, and Haran; and Haran was the father of Lot. Haran died before his father Terah in the land of his birth, in Ur of the Chaldeans... Terah took his son Abram and his grandson Lot son of Haran, and his daughter-in-law Sarai, his son Abram's wife, and they went out together from Ur of the Chaldeans to go into the land of Canaan; but when they came to Haran, they settled there. The days of Terah were two hundred and five years; and Terah died in Haran. Now the Lord said to Abram, 'Go from your country and your kindred and your father's house to the land that I will show you.

The calling of Abraham (as Abram became known) is one of the most famous Bible passages. If you start at Genesis 12, you gain the impression of a dramatic conversion—as if God called Abraham out of stability into a nomadic journey. Wind back a little, though, and you find that this is not quite the case; the search for the promised land had already begun.

Abraham's story belongs to a time of migrations in the Near East. He spent his early adulthood on the move, heading for Canaan, but, half-way there, he made a brief stop in Haran that somehow stretched on. God's call, some years later, was not out of the blue. The death of his father opened the way for reassessment. Abraham heard God's call and continued the journey he began in his youth.

Dramatic conversions are unusual. For most of us, the catalysing moments of calling lead us to fulfil what lies undiscovered at the centre of our being. Perhaps it is something that was cut off by circumstances—discouraging teachers, broken relationships, loss of confidence, finances, domestic responsibilities and more.

God does not usually call us in the opposite direction from where we were headed, but the call often pulls us out of what we've settled for, reignites our dreams and puts us back in touch with a sense of vocation that got buried along the way.

Prayer
God of all goodness, help me to rediscover my calling and to know it is never too late.

MAGGI DAWN

I will bless her

God said to Abraham, 'As for Sarai your wife, you shall not call her Sarai, but Sarah shall be her name. I will bless her, and moreover I will give you a son by her. I will bless her, and she shall give rise to nations; kings of peoples shall come from her.'… The angel of God called to Hagar from heaven, and said to her, 'What troubles you, Hagar? Do not be afraid; for God has heard the voice of the boy where he is. Come, lift up the boy and hold him fast with your hand, for I will make a great nation of him.'

For many people, reading the stories of the patriarchs—Abraham, Isaac and Jacob—is difficult precisely because they are 'patriarchal'. The heroes are nearly always men and it is easy for this to reinforce outdated gender stereotypes. For that reason, these verses jump right off the page to me.

We are familiar with God's call to Abraham—that God would bless him and make him the father of many nations—but here God says he will bless Sarah. The beginning of the salvation story prefigures its eventual fulfilment in Christ, born of a woman. Both the old and new covenants begin with mother and son embodying God's blessing and promise.

Later, when Sarah callously sends Ishmael and Hagar into the desert to die (21:9–14), God refuses to write them off as a mistake and again extends his promise that Ishmael, too, will be a father of nations. Christian history has often been inglorious in its exclusion of other traditions; we should never forget that, from the start, God's grace extends to those whom history locks out.

It would be extravagant to claim these accounts amount to anything like contemporary ideas of equality and justice. Nevertheless, in these scriptures, written down in contexts where women were customarily regarded as pieces of property, women are not excluded from the story. Here, I find glimmers of a God whose justice, fairness and love—then and now—cut through the inequities of mainstream culture.

Prayer

God of justice, help us to overcome prejudice and be bold enough to stand up for those who are marginalised in our churches.

MAGGI DAWN

God's table

The Lord appeared to Abraham by the oaks of Mamre... He looked up and saw three men standing near him... [and] ran from the tent entrance to meet them, and bowed down to the ground. He said, 'My lord, if I find favour with you, do not pass by your servant. Let a little water be brought, and wash your feet, and rest yourselves under the tree. Let me bring a little bread, that you may refresh yourselves, and after that you may pass on—since you have come to your servant.'... Abraham ran to the herd, and took a calf, tender and good, and gave it to the servant, who hastened to prepare it. Then he took curds and milk and the calf that he had prepared, and set it before them; and he stood by them under the tree while they ate.

I love this story of Abraham's table. It is not quite clear at what point Abraham realised his visitors were heavenly and not human figures, as his actions were standard nomadic hospitality. Then, as the meal unfolds and as they go walking after the meal, something shifts in the dynamic. It seems that although Abraham was the host, he was the one who was invited to God's table.

My own existence has been nomadic of late, having had five homes in two countries over the last two years, but, wherever I land, I love to invite people in. My rooms are often filled with students, but, rather than feeling that it costs me something, I feel rich as they fill up the rooms with their laughter and conversation. Many friendships have been forged in the kitchens of houses I have lived in.

Offering an open door to people passing through seems to me to be the most holy of gifts. Hospitality is a point at which I experience a curious reversal of social and spiritual dynamics. When I take things I consider to be my own and use them to serve others, I nearly always find myself feeling like a guest sitting at God's table.

Prayer

God of hospitality, bless our homes with joy and generosity, that your presence may be found by all who visit us.

MAGGI DAWN

Wednesday 1 October
Exodus 33:18–23 (NRSV)

A sound of God

Moses said, 'Show me your glory, I pray.' And [the Lord] said, 'I will make all my goodness pass before you, and will proclaim before you the name, "The Lord"; and I will be gracious to whom I will be gracious, and will show mercy on whom I will show mercy. But,' he said, 'you cannot see my face; for no one shall see me and live.' And the Lord continued, 'See, there is a place by me where you shall stand on the rock; and while my glory passes by I will put you in a cleft of the rock, and I will cover you with my hand until I have passed by; then I will take away my hand, and you shall see my back; but my face shall not be seen.'

I have sometimes envied people who say they can feel God's presence, because it never seems to work like that for me. Maybe that is why this is one of my favourite stories—where Moses, God's faithful servant and friend, is frustrated because he cannot see God. John Mason captured the same kind of longing in his poem, 'How shall I sing that majesty':

Thy brightness unto them appears,
whilst I thy footsteps trace;
a sound of God comes to my ears,
but they behold thy face.

No one can see God and live, Moses is told, but he does see God's disappearing back. The fourth-century theologian Gregory of Nazianzus described this as being 'like dappled reflections of sunlight on water, which reveal it to our dim eyes because we cannot look at the sun itself'.

We cannot see God, but we can see where God has been. When I see deep goodness in extraordinary acts of grace, find strength beyond my own to endure life's sorrows, or encounter unexpected gifts of friendship or something sublime through art or music, it is these things that are the sound of God to me. Whenever these happen, it seems that I look up and see God's tail lights glowing red on the horizon.

Prayer
God of mystery, help us to have faith even when we cannot see you clearly.

MAGGI DAWN

40

A mother in Israel

Then Deborah… sang on that day, saying: '… Hear, O kings; give ear, O princes; to the Lord I will sing, I will make melody to the Lord, the God of Israel. Lord, when you went out from Seir, when you marched from the region of Edom, the earth trembled, and the heavens poured, the clouds indeed poured water. The mountains quaked before the Lord, the One of Sinai, before the Lord, the God of Israel… The stars fought from heaven, from their courses they fought against Sisera. The torrent Kishon swept them away, the onrushing torrent, the torrent Kishon.'

The song of Deborah belongs to the time when the Bronze Age began to give way to the Iron Age, sparking a period of migration and unrest in the Mediterranean and Near East. The Pharaohs still ruled in Egypt and the Trojan War would soon break out, yet here we find the story of a majestic female chieftain.

I love the story of a woman who leads God's people as part of ancient tradition. I also love the way Deborah does not take all the credit herself but gives credit to others—men who promoted her and other women who contributed to her success, such as Jael, who slew a dangerous enemy not in battle but by conspiracy (v. 6). Deborah is poetic in her personification of natural features—clouds pouring water, stars fighting and a river going into battle. If she was such a good songwriter, though, why do we not have more of her songs, in Psalms, for instance?

Deborah's song was a favourite of Samuel Taylor Coleridge, who thought it was a sublime poem. He believed her eloquence to have been inspired purely by the intensity of the moment. The song's subject matter is passionate and can authentically be sung only by the author. Coleridge distinguished between this and the habitual poet, who crafts words that may not be intensely passionate or momentous but still speak the truth of life. Writing one good song, then, doesn't necessarily make you an artist, but every person has a song to sing.

Prayer
God of inspiration, help me to find my voice and be able to write or say or sing your praises.

MAGGI DAWN

1 Kings 19:4–8 (NRSV, abridged)

Eat, drink, sleep

[Elijah] went a day's journey into the wilderness, and came and sat down under a solitary broom tree. He asked that he might die: 'It is enough; now, O Lord, take away my life…' Then he lay down under the broom tree and fell asleep. Suddenly an angel touched him and said to him, 'Get up and eat.' He looked, and there at his head was a cake baked on hot stones, and a jar of water. He ate and drank, and lay down again. The angel of the Lord came a second time, touched him, and said, 'Get up and eat, otherwise the journey will be too much for you.' He got up, and ate and drank; then he went in the strength of that food for forty days and forty nights.

Most people know the story of Elijah triumphing over the Baal worshippers on the mountainside. Most people also remember him discovering in a remote cave that the voice of God was not in the earthquake, wind or fire, but in the still small voice. My favourite part of the story, however, lies between these two events.

After the mountainside events, Elijah is exhausted and has lost his perspective. He badly needs to hear God speak. First, though, God sends an angel with three gifts—not instructions nor demands, not more supernatural powers, but three ordinary things: food, drink and sleep.

In my last college, we told this story over and over again—usually in February, at the moment in the academic year when students were most worn out and despondent. We made a 'desert' in the chapel with a carpet of hessian and a thick layer of sand. We put a large, spiky pot plant in the middle and, at the base, a big goblet full of juice and a fruit cake. Propped against the bottom of the tree was this story of cake and sleep. I did not always see the students come and go, but, at intervals through each day, I would find the cake eaten and little notes of thanks pushed into the sand.

Reflection

Sometimes, when we are stressed, we imagine we need more strength, more prayer, more stamina and more wisdom. Perhaps, like Elijah, we just first need the angel's gifts: eat, drink, sleep.

Maggi Dawn

Pleasant places

A Miktam of David. Protect me, O God, for in you I take refuge. I say to the Lord, 'You are my Lord; I have no good apart from you.' … The boundary lines have fallen for me in pleasant places; I have a goodly heritage… Therefore my heart is glad, and my soul rejoices; my body also rests secure. For you do not give me up to Sheol, or let your faithful one see the Pit. You show me the path of life. In your presence there is fullness of joy; in your right hand are pleasures for evermore.

'A Miktam of David' is usually in small print in English Bibles, as if it were an explanatory note, but, in Hebrew, it is part of the text. No one is certain what 'miktam' means, but six psalms open with this word. All are psalms of lament; four of them concern David's struggles with his enemies.

The joyful words of verses 6 and 11, then, were written while the psalmist was in a situation of bodily threat. He recalls God's blessings to sustain his sense of joy under duress. It is too easy to assume that joy is only available in the good times. This Miktam reminds us that, while belonging to God does not save us from conflict or struggle, we are not defined by these things alone.

Years later, Nehemiah wrote that 'the joy of the Lord is your strength' (8:10). He, too, knew that to discover joy in tribulation is what we need to do to sustain us. Scientific studies have shown that joy increases measurably when words of gratitude are spoken aloud. Joy is not an emotion that descends when the pressure is off, but a sustaining knowledge of goodness that we cultivate through the practice of thanksgiving.

For me, practising joy has become a habit of life. If I deliberately find something to rejoice about in dark times, it is a profound source of strength and, on occasion, has saved me from sinking into despair. Even at an everyday level, practising joy can bring energy to a flat day.

Prayer
God of joy, teach us to be thankful and to take joy in the small things.

MAGGI DAWN

Loud cymbals

Praise the Lord! Praise God in his sanctuary; praise him in the mighty firmament! Praise him for his mighty deeds; praise him according to his surpassing greatness! Praise him with trumpet sound; praise him with lute and harp! Praise him with tambourine and dance; praise him with strings and pipe! Praise him with clanging cymbals; praise him with loud clashing cymbals! Let everything that breathes praise the Lord! Praise the Lord!

Anyone who has been involved in church music will be familiar with the arguments that surround it. I am a guitarist and have often encountered uneasiness about whether or not guitars are suitable for worship. I have even been told that the 'right' instrument for worship is a pipe organ. I was amused, then, when I read that pipe organs were mostly removed during the Reformation and, when they were reintroduced in the 17th century, there was an outcry over the unholy noise they made! It is interesting how quick we are to deem familiar music as 'holy' and other music as unsuitable for church, when the scriptures tell us a different story.

Evidence suggests that the early Christians did not use instruments in worship, in a deliberate attempt to make their worship distinct from that of other religions, but the orchestra the psalmist describes here includes strings, trumpets and wind instruments, along with clanging cymbals. The 'trumpets' were probably animal horns, which can make a dramatic sound. It seems that some of the percussionists were expected to dance, too, as they played. The psalmist, then, is describing for us a visual feast as well as loud music—a swaying, dancing band of musicians and not a row of angelic, barely moving choirboys.

Beyond a few guesses, we cannot be sure how this ancient music, or that of the early church, actually sounded. At least we have this indication that it was boldly, unashamedly noisy! When I plug in my guitar or my bass, I am glad that we have the psalmist's mandate not to be afraid of loud noise and music that makes you move your feet.

Prayer

God of the dance, help me to be generous in welcoming different forms of worship and unashamed about giving thanks to you.

MAGGI DAWN

Perfect peace

Thou dost keep him in perfect peace, whose mind is stayed on thee, because he trusts in thee. Trust in the Lord for ever, for the Lord God is an everlasting rock.

A long time ago, when I first encountered the Christian faith, a girl at my school gave me a slip of paper on which she had written these verses from Isaiah. I had exams coming up and, although I was not nervous, she was and she thought I should be too. 'Learn this by heart,' she said. 'Then, while you are waiting to turn over the paper and start the exam, just say it to yourself in your head. It really helps to keep you calm.'

To this day, in moments of stress I find myself reciting these same words to myself. The image of God as a rock and the poetic rhythm of the words steady my nerves and make me breathe in and out again, safe in the knowledge that there is strength beyond my own.

Memorising scripture is not fashionable today, but I am glad I learned to do it (along with memorising poetry), despite the awkwardness of never being able to get my mouth around the latest translation. For me, these verses always come out of my mouth in the words of the Revised Standard Version of the Bible because that is the version I learned. It has never occurred to me to rephrase them as, 'keep *her* in perfect peace'. The timeless quality of the poetry seems to do its work without needing to particularise it. Its truth seems more timeless because it is not adapted to suit me.

Later, I discovered these verses appear in the midst of a violent passage, written to strengthen people dealing with situations infinitely more stressful than sitting an exam. They need their minds to be 'stayed'—that is, tethered securely—on God under unimaginable pressure. I am glad I learned in manageable circumstances to focus my mind on the rock-like quality of God, to find peace and calm beyond myself. It is a lesson that later carried me through stress I would not have believed possible when I was 15.

Prayer

God of peace, I commit my day to you. Keep me in perfect peace; stay my mind on you.

MAGGI DAWN

Slow harvest

That same day Jesus went out of the house and sat beside the lake. Such great crowds gathered around him that he got into a boat and sat there, while the crowd stood on the beach. And he told them many things in parables, saying: 'Listen! A sower went out to sow. And… some seeds fell on the path, and the birds came and ate them up. Other seeds fell on rocky ground, where they did not have much soil, and they sprang up quickly, since they had no depth of soil. But when the sun rose, they were scorched; and since they had no root, they withered away. Other seeds fell among thorns, and the thorns grew up and choked them. Other seeds fell on good soil and brought forth grain, some a hundredfold, some sixty, some thirty. Let anyone with ears listen!'

The Gospels say that Jesus often went off by himself—sometimes in the mountains, sometimes all night—usually to pray. Here, though, he is not praying—he is doing nothing at all. This, for me, is the lens through which to read the parable that follows.

The crowd interrupts his reverie, wanting more of his time, stories and attention, but when they get what they want from him, where does it go? Some goes nowhere, some takes root but grows too fast and dies, and some is crowded out and starves. The slow, steady growth of the life he gives them needs time and space that only a few will give it.

Sporadic attention is not enough. Growth has to be protected from competing interests and have space and time to develop. Instant results may look good, but you cannot rush spiritual growth.

To my eye, this is more a parable about us than about mission. If you want spiritual life, you have to do what Jesus did regularly—slow down and do nothing. We live in a world where doing nothing is increasingly less likely—we can be connected even in our downtime and absorbing information while we are running or working out. How often do we do nothing?

Prayer

God of the harvest, help me to enjoy the slow pace of growth and not lose heart.

MAGGI DAWN

Back to the start

As [Mary Magdalene, Mary the mother of James, and Salome] entered the tomb, they saw a young man, dressed in a white robe, sitting on the right side; and they were alarmed. But he said to them, 'Do not be alarmed; you are looking for Jesus of Nazareth, who was crucified. He has been raised; he is not here. Look, there is the place they laid him. But go, tell his disciples and Peter that he is going ahead of you to Galilee; there you will see him, just as he told you.' So they went out and fled from the tomb, for terror and amazement had seized them; and they said nothing to anyone, for they were afraid.

I love novels with surprise endings, two alternative conclusions or a revelation that suddenly shifts the sense of the story. Mark's Gospel is like this. Many scholars think the original Gospel ended at the point in verse 8 given above, but, because Mark barely hinted at a resurrection, editors added on extra verses to 'complete' the story—a short ending (v. 8b) and a long one (vv. 9–20).

Mark, though, was a smarter author than his editors gave him credit for. Unusual endings are there to elicit a response. In this case, if you stop at verse 8, you read an account full of unresolved energy. The mysterious figure at the tomb tells the three women to go and tell and not to be afraid. What do they do? They are yet more terrified, run away, and tell no one. The story stops abruptly rather than giving a satisfying sense of closure. This, though, takes the reader right back to the beginning of Mark's Gospel to revisit all the places where Jesus says secretively, 'Don't tell anyone who I am.' There is a hint that the secret is out in these final verses—but, to discover it, the reader must go back and look again.

The truth of the resurrection only comes into focus when we reread the story and begin to realise, as Mark tells it, that it is not really about the disciples but about us.

Prayer

God of surprises, thank you for the imaginative writers who brought us the Gospels. Help me to be an imaginative reader.

MAGGI DAWN

The girl and the woman

Now when Jesus returned, the crowd welcomed him, for they were all waiting for him. Just then there came a man named Jairus, a leader of the synagogue. He fell at Jesus' feet and begged him to come to his house, for he had an only daughter, about twelve years old, who was dying. As he went, the crowds pressed in on him. Now there was a woman who had been suffering from haem-orrhages for twelve years; and though she had spent all she had on physicians, no one could cure her. She came up behind him and touched the fringe of his clothes, and immediately her haem-orrhage stopped. Then Jesus asked, 'Who touched me?'

Here, we have two stories of healing by Jesus, woven together so that layers of meaning emerge. The girl was 12, the age when girls became women. She had all the privileges that a woman of the time could have had—youth, wealth, marriageability—but she fell ill and was dying.

On his way to heal her, another woman interrupted Jesus, and the connections between their two stories are striking. The girl had privi-leges; the woman had none. The girl was on the brink of womanhood; the woman's gynaecological problems made her an outcast. The girl was young and wealthy; the woman was older and owned nothing. The girl had a father who could ask for anything she needed; the woman did not belong to anyone and had no right to ask for help. Also, the woman had been ill for twelve years—the length of time the girl had been alive.

Did Jesus have his priorities the wrong way around? Was it not more urgent to heal the dying child than care for the older woman? Apparently he thought not. Giving proper dignity to the woman was part of her healing. The privileged child had to wait while the woman's needs were met. The humanising quality of this encounter with an unknown woman, who was nobody's wife and nobody's daughter, is one of the most profound stories of God's kindness in the Bible.

Prayer

God of kindness, thank you that you notice the downtrodden. Today we pray for those who have no one to pray for them.

MAGGI DAWN

JOHN 18:15–17 (NRSV)

Outside looking in

Simon Peter and another disciple followed Jesus. Since that disciple was known to the high priest, he went with Jesus into the courtyard of the high priest, but Peter was standing outside at the gate. So the other disciple, who was known to the high priest, went out, spoke to the woman who guarded the gate, and brought Peter in. The woman said to Peter, 'You are not also one of this man's disciples, are you?' He said, 'I am not.'

Why did Peter, of all people, deny Christ? It was out of character for him; he was a consistently loyal friend who was never afraid to speak up even when others did not. Perhaps the answer lies in what happens to Peter immediately beforehand. Step back for a minute to look at his experience.

They approach the gated house of a powerful member of society. The owner of the house knows the first disciple and, as the doors open, he enters with a small crowd. Peter does not know the high priest and is left outside. The first disciple later returns with permission to let him in, but, even then, Peter gets only as far as the courtyard while his friend goes into the inner room with the important people.

How must it have felt to see the other disciple gain instant access while he was left outside? We often forget that most of the disciples had already fled that night. Peter acted entirely out of his comfort zone to stay close to Jesus. It was only when he found himself left out that he retreated, losing all his characteristic bluster and confidence.

The story of Peter's denial of Christ is often told as a cautionary tale, as if to help us avoid making the same mistake. It seems to me that we cannot avoid such mistakes, but this story shows that even when we get things terribly wrong and lose our confidence, we can still be put back together and even end up leading the Church!

Prayer

God of faithfulness, thank you for holding on even when life's circumstances trip me up. Help me to know I am loved and not left out.

MAGGI DAWN

A theological puzzle

Let the same mind be in you that was in Christ Jesus, who, though he was in the form of God, did not regard equality with God as something to be exploited, but emptied himself, taking the form of a slave, being born in human likeness... He humbled himself and became obedient to the point of death—even death on a cross. Therefore God also highly exalted him and gave him the name that is above every name, so that at the name of Jesus every knee should bend, in heaven and on earth and under the earth, and every tongue should confess that Jesus Christ is Lord, to the glory of God the Father.

This brief passage may have been a quote from an early Christian hymn. Although the meaning is very dense, two ideas stand out. The first is that Jesus 'empties himself'. This is more than merely giving up heavenly status to become human. This act of self-emptying represents a complete giving, not merely of status but also the whole self, for the benefit of others. This risky level of generosity is what characterises God's love and Christ's action in his incarnation. Thus, a short poetic phrase delivers an enormous theological idea in a nutshell. Like any good song, its condensed poetic language contains layers of meaning.

The second idea evokes a theological puzzle. The trajectory of the passage has Jesus starting out 'in the form of God' and having 'equality with God'. What could be more exalted than that? Yet, at the end, it says that God 'highly exalted him', implying that, because of his great act of self-giving love, Jesus ended up in an even higher state of glory than when he began. Here is the puzzle, then: how could he end up in a higher place than where he started—equality with God? It is a puzzle with no satisfactory answer, a mystery to ponder. It is far more enjoyable to be intrigued by possible solutions than find quick, easy answers.

Prayer

God of all wisdom, thank you for the beauty of poetry, the fascination of intellectual puzzles and the joy of knowing that our pursuit of understanding will never come to an end.

MAGGI DAWN

Corinthian Christians

1 and 2 Corinthians are probably the edited contents of several shorter letters from Paul to the church in the Greek city of Corinth. They are some of the earliest documents in the Christian story, dating to the early 50s AD, so they cast light on the nature of the movement that grew up around the memory of Jesus while there were still people around who had known him. The experience of Paul's own mystical encounter with the risen Jesus on the road to Damascus also shines through them.

These letters are set in a particular context. Corinth was the provincial capital of the Roman province of Achaia and a key interconnecting point for government, travel and trade. We can imagine that the letters therefore give us an indication of what it was like to be a community of followers of the Jesus Way in the Roman Empire, away from the Jewish homeland of the God-man at the centre of the story. Now, this context is not our context. Part of the challenge, then, is to read instructions and advice for a setting very different from our own and imagine what they might have to say to us now.

Unlike some other of the Pauline letters, 1 and 2 Corinthians are not primarily theological treatises, but practical messages addressing particular issues that have arisen in the church. The theology is there, of course, sometimes up front but often hidden. Perhaps in those moments the task is to mine for the theology that lies beneath the surface of the first-century Roman Empire context and bring it out in our own contexts. The practical outworking of the theology may or may not look similar to what was happening in Corinth.

Inevitably, in just two weeks we will only be able to focus on very small segments of the letters. If you can, try to make space to read the letters through in one or two sittings. If at times they can seem very familiar, they can also be full of surprises. There is great strength and comfort in them, but they may also provoke unease, awkwardness and even anger. Whatever the case, we will not be left unchanged.

Ian Adams

(Re)discover your calling!

Paul, called to be an apostle of Christ Jesus by the will of God, and our brother Sosthenes. To the church of God that is in Corinth, to those who are sanctified in Christ Jesus, called to be saints, together with all those who in every place call on the name of our Lord Jesus Christ, both their Lord and ours: Grace to you and peace from God our Father and the Lord Jesus Christ.

Right at the beginning of this series of letters, as we have them, is a theme with the potential to change everything: the gift to each of us of God's calling. Paul identifies himself as one called to be an apostle of Christ Jesus by the will of God. This letter, he says, is written to the church in Corinth, to those called to be saints. The times in which Paul wrote were challenging. In many parts of the Roman Empire it was proving very dangerous to be a follower of Jesus, but it was this sense of divine calling that kept Paul in his mission, despite the huge challenges he faced. It is this sense of divine calling, he seems to suggest, that will keep the tender young Christian community in Corinth through all the things that threatened to destabilise and throw it off course.

So, a question for you and me: what do you sense may be your divine calling at this time? Can you begin to describe it? In my experience, the core of our calling tends to remain pretty constant. The way it looks and the ways in which it is worked out will evolve over time, as we change and the context in which we live evolves. Our callings will need to be made real—to be incarnated—in particular times and particular places, but the essence will remain the same: to live the gospel story where we are, drawing on our own unique mix of gifts, experience and yearning.

Prayer

May you discover a renewed sense of God's calling to you. May you find yourself in the stream of God's grace and peace.

Ian Adams

Agreement or division?

Now I appeal to you, brothers and sisters, by the name of our Lord Jesus Christ, that all of you should be in agreement and that there should be no divisions among you, but that you should be united in the same mind and the same purpose. For it has been reported to me by Chloe's people that there are quarrels among you, my brothers and sisters.

The scene has been set by Paul at the start of this letter, a solid base for all that will follow: the importance of a sense of God's calling, a blessing for grace and peace, thanksgiving for the church in Corinth and a reminder of God's faithfulness. Now, we could say, to business!

Item number one on the agenda is the choice in the church between agreement and division. Arguments and quarrels have clearly become a big enough issue in the Corinthian church for Paul to mention it from the start. The precise nature of these quarrels does not matter at this stage. What is clear for Paul is that these disagreements have become corrosive. You need, he urges, to be of the same mind and same purpose.

Divisions and quarrels are, of course, part of what happens when we human beings engage in some collective task. They go with the territory. We cannot act as if they do not (or should not) exist. Differences will arise. What we can and must do, however, is to work out how to address them and make sure that this process becomes part of the way we live out our calling.

So, how to do this? Any real change must begin with us as individuals. If there is division around, perhaps we need to begin by reflecting on our own part in the issue. Then we may find ourselves in a position to engage in the vital (if difficult) conversations with our brothers and sisters that will need to take place.

Reflection

Am I helping the emergence of a common mind and purpose in my context? How might I need to change to enable unity to emerge? What might be a first step towards finding a new sense of common mind and purpose for all involved?

IAN ADAMS

Mystery in the ordinary

When I came to you, brothers and sisters, I did not come proclaiming the mystery of God to you in lofty words or wisdom. For I decided to know nothing among you except Jesus Christ, and him crucified. And I came to you in weakness and in fear and in much trembling.

How might God be encountered? Paul suggests here that words matter in opening up the path to encounter (and how brilliant are the words he uses in the many letters he writes to the churches). Wisdom, too, is a beautiful and revelatory thing (and it is enlightening to see how sensitively and imaginatively Paul engages with the wisdom traditions of his time). For Paul, though, Jesus Christ is to be encountered primarily 'among you'. Mystery is to be encountered in the ordinary, found in and among us, discovered in the here and now.

What is particularly interesting about Paul's emphasis here is that we might have expected something very different from one whose life had been so shaped by some extraordinarily mystical experiences—his Damascus road encounter with the risen Jesus and his experience of being 'caught up to the third heaven' (an experience that he speaks of in the third person but is almost certainly his own, in 2 Corinthians 12:2). We might have imagined that he would urge others to pursue similar experiences, but no. It is, he says, in the flesh-and-blood nature of community, in our encounters with each other, that Christ is to be found.

It is surely no accident that here Paul speaks of the crucified Christ. Community can sometimes be a beautiful experience, but most of the time it is pretty ordinary. Sometimes it can be tough and, sad to say, occasionally it can even be brutal—a kind of crucifixion. Whatever our community is like at this time—beautiful, ordinary or tough—this may be the place, suggests Paul, where Christ can be found.

Prayer

Crucified Christ, I pray that you will give me all the insight, courage and love I will need today to know you in the communities of which I am part. May others also see something of you in me.

Ian Adams

The small ingredient

Do you not know that a little yeast leavens the whole batch of dough? Clean out the old yeast so that you may be a new batch, as you really are unleavened. For our paschal lamb, Christ, has been sacrificed. Therefore, let us celebrate the festival, not with the old yeast, the yeast of malice and evil, but with the unleavened bread of sincerity and truth.

This is part of a longer passage dealing with another major issue that has arisen in the church at Corinth—a case of sexual immorality in which a man is 'living with his father's wife' (5:1). Whatever the detail (and the implication is that incest is involved), this is almost certainly just one strand in a much wider issue for the church—how to live in a society where sex has commonly become detached from long-term commitment and other generally accepted boundaries.

In various places in these letters Paul's condemnation of immoral behaviour is clear. In a sense it is easy to be proscriptive. 'That is wrong—do not do it.' Interestingly, in this short passage the case Paul makes to the church in Corinth is a positive one. They are called to live a different way, to be the yeast that leavens the whole batch of dough, to live out the sacrifice made by the Christ. So, if we behave differently, it is not just a negative protest but a positive attempt to live the way of Christ quietly within society and play our part in a deeper change for good in the wider world.

Dealing with immoral behaviour has sometimes brought out the worst in church communities. Trapped between our best aspirations and our messy realities, church has from time to time been the setting for words and actions that have not truly reflected the demanding but compassionate ways of Jesus. This is perhaps why Paul says that the church at Corinth is not to act from malice or evil, but with sincerity and truth.

Prayer

Jesus, help me today to be a small ingredient for good, to live with sincerity and truth and so help bring your deep change to the world around me.

IAN ADAMS

More than knowledge, love

> Now concerning food sacrificed to idols: we know that 'all of us possess knowledge'. Knowledge puffs up, but love builds up. Anyone who claims to know something does not yet have the necessary knowledge; but anyone who loves God is known by him.

Knowledge or love may at first seem to be a strange choice. Why is it not possible to have both? We should remember that the context of this part of 1 Corinthians is a conversation about the eating of food that has been offered to idols. The knowledge that Paul is referring to seems to be that of church members who 'know' that, while such food is inappropriate for consumption, their freedom in Christ means they can eat such food if they wish. Paul agrees with their correctness in principle, but, in practice—and with those in mind whom he terms 'weaker' in faith—he suggests that something may be more important than this knowledge.

While knowledge certainly matters, I think Paul is criticising what may be done with such knowledge. In a neat play with words, he writes that while knowledge puffs up, love builds up. On its own, knowledge is just about knowing things. What is important is what we do with that knowledge, how we hold it, how we share it and how we live in the light of it. Without love, knowledge is next to worthless. In fact, if ever we claim to know something fully we are immediately rumbled: 'Anyone who claims to know something does not yet have the necessary knowledge' (v. 2). All our knowledge is limited, so it is never possible to be fully right. How perceptive is Paul!

The final phrase in this brief passage hints at how love and knowledge can truly come together. Love God, says Paul, and we will be known by God—a knowing that is far more than head knowledge, a knowing that encompasses intimacy, acceptance and love without limit.

Reflection

Reflect on the place that knowledge plays within you. How are you holding it, sharing it and living in the light of it at this time? How could your knowledge build up?

IAN ADAMS

1 Corinthians 11:4–5 (NRSV)

Honour God in your context

Any man who prays or prophesies with something on his head
disgraces his head, but any woman who prays or prophesies with
her head unveiled disgraces her head—it is one and the same
thing as having her head shaved.

Here we step into awkward territory. Much of this passage (vv. 2–16)
sits extremely uneasily with the way many of us live now, and I am not
going to attempt to smooth away those difficulties in my brief com-
ments here. It is a debate about head coverings, possibly aimed at helping the church at Corinth understand how people should, in their dress
for worship, reflect or reject the practices of other religions and cults in
wider society. Here, Paul makes an argument for head coverings for
females and none for males, based on his understanding that 'Christ is
the head of every man, and the husband is the head of his wife, and
God is the head of Christ' (v. 3)—and that man 'is the image and reflection of God; but woman is the reflection of man' (v. 7).

This argument may feel strange to many of us and perhaps all we can
do with the strangeness is remember that the society and culture inhab-
ited by Paul and the Corinthian church were very different from those
in which most people reading these notes today live.

I would suggest that we mine for the theology that lies behind Paul's
instructions. When we do this, perhaps what emerges as truly important here are two ideas. First, our physicality in worship matters. It is
not just about words; we bring all of our self to prayer and worship—
and our worship practices need to reflect that.

Second, we need to reflect on our place as would-be Christ followers
within wider society. To what extent do we amend our ways of being to
'fit in', and when are we happy to remain distinctive? The details that
emerge from such conversations will no doubt differ from community
to community, church to church, individual to individual. What matters
is that the reflection is authentic.

Reflection

How may you bring your physical presence to prayer today?

Ian Adams

Wait for one another

> So then, my brothers and sisters, when you come together to eat,
> wait for one another. If you are hungry, eat at home, so that when
> you come together, it will not be for your condemnation. About the
> other things I will give instructions when I come.

Here, Paul addresses the practice of celebrating the Lord's Supper. It is
interesting to see in such an early document how important this act
already was in the life of the church.

There was a problem in Corinth. The practice of the Supper had
clearly become unruly. It seems as if the liturgy that had accompanied
the meal since its inception was in danger of being lost: some people
were getting drunk and others treating the supper as a free meal, finish-
ing before others had even arrived. Such happenings were proving
destructive, to the point where Paul made a link between these abuses
and the illness and even deaths of some in the community.

It is unlikely (I hope) that any of the above are issues in your church
community, but the place of the Lord's Supper (Holy Communion,
Eucharist or Mass) and our attitude towards it are key in the life of any
community that follows Christ. Of course, various traditions within the
church have different emphases when it comes to Communion, but
Paul's focus here is one that is, I think, common and vital to all. Paul
asks the Corinthian Christians to wait for each other and so honour the
body—the community—which is the body of Christ. The instruction to
'examine yourselves' is primarily about community, not the individual.
Essentially, before we eat and drink, we should ask ourselves if we have
made peace with each other as far as we can.

In this context, Paul's instruction to 'wait for one another' is not just
an issue of politeness but also an impassioned plea to guard the life of
the community. Communion is not just an individual encounter but also
a making of community. For Paul, therefore, some other issues can wait
(for which 'I will give instructions when I come'), but this is urgent.

Reflection

*In the wider context of this day, what might 'waiting for one another' look
like for you?*

IAN ADAMS

Love, above all

If I speak in the tongues of mortals and of angels, but do not have love, I am a noisy gong or a clanging cymbal. And if I have prophetic powers, and understand all mysteries and all knowledge, and if I have all faith, so as to remove mountains, but do not have love, I am nothing. If I give away all my possessions, and if I hand over my body so that I may boast, but do not have love, I gain nothing.

This brilliant passage from Paul is so familiar to us (and a particular favourite at weddings) that it is very interesting to try to see it back in its original context—a small first-century Christ-following community in a very challenging environment.

The inference is clear. In the church at Corinth some pretty impressive patterns of life and worship had been emerging, but Paul found something missing. Ecstatic tongues, prophetic powers, understanding of mystery, deep faith, great generosity and even sacrificial willingness to accept suffering were all present. This was all to be commended, but the key to it all looked as if it was being lost. These commendable ways of being were in danger of becoming just so much more noise in a noisy city at a noisy time—like gongs, like clanging cymbals. It was all surface, with no depth; all show, no reality.

Paul could see what was missing and homed in on it. 'I may have all this,' he says (and how gracious that he included himself in this image, too), but 'if I do not have love, I am nothing.' Without love, all our words and actions (even the very best ones) come to nothing. It is all about love!

There is a link here with the great conclusion that the young disciple John came to. If we take him to be the author of the Gospel and the letters, he wrote towards the end of his life that 'God is love' (1 John 4:8). Forget almost everything else, say Paul and John; love is what truly matters. How liberating and full of possibility!

Prayer

Jesus of the church of Corinth, Jesus of Paul, Jesus of John, enable the beautiful sound of love to resound in me today.

Ian Adams

1 Corinthians 15:12–14 (NRSV)

Resurrection people

> Now if Christ is proclaimed as raised from the dead, how can some of you say there is no resurrection of the dead? If there is no resurrection of the dead, then Christ has not been raised; and if Christ has not been raised, then our proclamation has been in vain and your faith has been in vain.

Another big issue has arisen in the church at Corinth, which cuts to the heart of the memory of Jesus and the community that is growing around that memory. It seems that some in the church are saying that the resurrection of the dead is impossible and, by inference, they are doubting the resurrection of Jesus.

For Paul, the resurrection of Jesus is absolutely central to his faith. It is also highly personal. 'Last of all,' Paul writes, 'as to one untimely born, he [Jesus] appeared also to me' (15:8). Without his resurrection, he says to the Corinthians, all our proclamations and all your faith is in vain. In the verses that follow, Paul sets out reasons for his belief in the resurrection of Jesus, shows how it offers grounds for believing in the resurrection of the saints and beautifully imagines what the final resurrection might be like: 'Just as we have borne the image of the man of dust, we will also bear the image of the man of heaven' (v. 49).

So, what is the resurrection to us? As Paul makes clear to the Corinthians, this is not just an academic exercise. For us, too, it is not just about a life beyond this earthly experience. Something changes when the resurrection of Jesus moves from a concept to a stepped-into, lived-out reality wherever we are. The resurrection of Jesus continues here and it continues now. This is the day to live resurrection! A new way of being, a new life, has become possible—and it needs to be lived now by us, his resurrection people.

Reflection

Reflect on the importance of Jesus' resurrection to you. How could you live today in the spirit of his resurrection and the hope it gives us? What might that feel like to you and how could it be a gift to others?

IAN ADAMS

Names, faces, people!

Now, brothers and sisters, you know that members of the household of Stephanas were the first converts in Achaia, and they have devoted themselves to the service of the saints; I urge you to put yourselves at the service of such people, and of everyone who works and toils with them. I rejoice at the coming of Stephanas and Fortunatus and Achaicus, because they have made up for your absence; for they refreshed my spirit as well as yours. So give recognition to such persons.

One of the great gifts of the Pauline letters is the way in which he constantly sprinkles them with references to the people of the church communities to, from and about which he is writing. This, for Paul, is how the gospel is lived out—in the lives, in the names and in the faces of people. So, he regularly concludes his letters with lots of personal references. Here, Stephanas, Fortunatus and Achaicus are given a mention, Timothy and Apollos have already featured (vv. 10–12) and Aquila and Prisca are about to appear, too (v. 19).

Our exploration of the heart of God invariably brings us back to something close to home, because good theology always has a human face. The people we are working with, living alongside and bumping into are the site of God's activity in the world. God is not to be sought in some perfect community, some dream church or some special neighbourhood, but is there to be discovered in the people around us and in the communities of which we are part, day by day.

It is in this context that Paul sets out the kinds of qualities that will be needed by followers of the Jesus Way: an appetite for devotion and service, work and toil, refreshment and greeting. This is not a spectacular life and it is not necessarily what we would prefer to hear, but it is the way that the great story is to be lived and shared.

Prayer

Jesus, I pray that you will help me this day to see your face in the faces of those around me; to hear your name in the names I speak; to receive your greeting in those I greet.

IAN ADAMS

What is that aroma?

> But thanks be to God, who in Christ always leads us in triumphal procession, and through us spreads in every place the fragrance that comes from knowing him. For we are the aroma of Christ to God among those who are being saved and among those who are perishing; to the one a fragrance from death to death, to the other a fragrance from life to life.

'We are the aroma of Christ' (v. 15) is one of Paul's most memorable metaphors for how the church might live and make a difference within society. He is almost certainly drawing on what would have been a vibrant and memorable experience in major centres of the Roman Empire—the triumphal procession, celebrating a victory for the empire and combining military might, civic honour and religious rite. The procession would have had a strong impact on all who saw it and participated in it.

Paul suggests that the life of the Corinthian church community could have a similar impact on all who encounter the church, and he picks up on a particular aspect of the procession. As the military triumph is accompanied by clouds of incense, providing a powerful sensory experience, so the Christ procession—the Christ path—is accompanied by a beautiful aroma, 'the fragrance that comes from knowing him' (v. 14).

For most of us the sense of smell is a powerful thing. A strange scent can make us inquisitive; a bad smell can make us gag; a beautiful aroma can draw us in. Interestingly, Paul suggests that the Christ aroma will produce very different reactions in people. To some it will be a fragrance of life, while to others it will seem to be a 'fragrance from death to death' (v. 16).

This is tough. We would love for everyone to respond to Jesus and his way with open hearts and open arms, but that, says Paul, will not always be the case. Our calling is to follow Christ, who leads the procession, and let him spread the fragrance of his presence to all around us.

Reflection

Think about what kind of aroma your life may produce today. How would you describe the aroma of Christ's presence?

Ian Adams

2 CORINTHIANS 4:7–10 (NRSV)

The authentic life

But we have this treasure in clay jars, so that it may be made clear that this extraordinary power belongs to God and does not come from us. We are afflicted in every way, but not crushed; perplexed, but not driven to despair; persecuted, but not forsaken; struck down, but not destroyed; always carrying in the body the death of Jesus, so that the life of Jesus may also be made visible in our bodies.

How can we keep going when everything around us seems to be falling apart? In an intensely personal passage, Paul sets out for the church at Corinth what it will be like to follow Jesus Christ in the often challenging setting of the Roman Empire. It may be, he says, that we are afflicted, perplexed, persecuted and struck down, but, through all this, we will not be crushed, not driven to despair, not forsaken, not destroyed. What is the reason for this extraordinary hope? It is the surprising presence and power of God in us and through it all, like treasure in humble clay jars. This is immensely encouraging. However weakened or beaten we may be feeling, God is close, God is good and God is enough.

What is particularly interesting about Paul's description of his experience (which very clearly emerges from his own life story) is his sense that, in some way, the death of Jesus is (and needs to be) visible in the followers of Jesus. Only in this way will the life of Jesus also be revealed in us. Encountering a Christian, we might say, is to meet someone who is clearly dying and at the same time clearly full of life. Now this may feel a bit conceptual—and how Paul loves a big concept—but there is a gritty reality to it. Our following of Christ must take us ever more into authenticity and transparency. Our (so-called) failures and losses are just as much part of the story as our (so-called) successes and gains. Death and life, every day.

Prayer

Jesus, give me courage to carry both your death and your life
in my body today.

IAN ADAMS

Open your hearts

> We have spoken frankly to you Corinthians; our heart is wide open to you. There is no restriction in our affections, but only in yours. In return—I speak as to children—open wide your hearts also.

Paul can do brilliant and sophisticated theologising. He creates magnificent ideas and paints pictures for life that echo through the centuries. His words, at various times compelling or disturbing, produce powerful reactions, but always he returns to human encounter. Open your hearts, he writes to the church at Corinth; embrace us as we embrace you.

Clearly there has been something of a breakdown in relations between some in the church and Paul, but he takes the first step towards renewing the relationship. This is a costly path. Paul feels let down by some people in the church, misunderstood by others, even betrayed in some cases. We can sense the pain in his defence of his ministry, but somehow he finds the grace to open himself up to those who have closed themselves off to him.

Time and time again in our exploration of 1 and 2 Corinthians we have seen how big theological ideas need to take shape in earthy human encounters. So, what might be the first step that we could take today to open up a relationship that has become closed?

Some self-awareness and soul-work may need to be done here. How easily we restrict our affections when we feel let down, perhaps reaching for the sanction of the 'silent treatment' and other similar responses, depending on our temperament. A conscious decision to remove the restriction in our affections is the beginning. As we do this, we may discover in God's gracious care that something beautiful begins to open up in us and, in time, in those to whom we had slowly become strangers. We may discover that, actually, this all happens very naturally—perhaps, as Paul hints, as if we were children, who have a wonderful capacity to be present to others.

Prayer

Compassionate Jesus, help me to remove the restrictions to my affections. Open my heart like a child's again, and open up the way to renewed relationships with those around me.

IAN ADAMS

2 Corinthians 13:11–13 (NRSV)

As simple—and as difficult—as this

Finally, brothers and sisters, farewell. Put things in order, listen to my appeal, agree with one another, live in peace; and the God of love and peace will be with you. Greet one another with a holy kiss. All the saints greet you. The grace of the Lord Jesus Christ, the love of God, and the communion of the Holy Spirit be with all of you.

Here we reach the end of the letters. So, this is what it comes down to. Put things right. Work out a common way forward. Live in peace. That is it—as simple, and as difficult, as that.

All of this, it seems, can be carried in a 'holy kiss'. At its best, this kiss is a sacrament of togetherness, of body, of community, of love—both symbolising the union of those kissing and at the same time deepening that union.

Now, a holy kiss clearly made sense in the context of Corinth and it might make sense for you if you are reading these notes in a culture where, perhaps, an exchange of kisses on the cheek is a regular part of daily life, a statement of respect and honour. If your culture is different (and in much of the UK, for example, that might be so) the question may be to work out together what such a gesture might be. What is the 'holy kiss' in our context, serving as a sacrament of our togetherness in Christ?

Paul concludes with a blessing: 'The grace of the Lord Jesus Christ, the love of God, and the communion of the Holy Spirit be with all of you' (v. 13). We are not alone in our attempts to bring goodness to the world and help shape it in the way of the kingdom of heaven. The Father's love, the Son's grace and the Spirit's close communion are all ours, each a holy kiss as we set out on a new stage of our journey with Christ. That will be enough.

Prayer
Father, Son and Holy Spirit, with your kiss I resume the journey. May I carry your love, grace and communion to all I encounter.

Ian Adams

The Age of the Saints

All Saints Day falls on 1 November and we traditionally remember the saints and martyrs of our various nations on 8 November, so, in the next couple of weeks, we shall rely on a number of saints to guide us in our reflections and prayers. We shall be focusing on the early phase of the remarkable missionary venture that rooted Christianity in the culture of people of the countries we now call Great Britain and Ireland. This means we shall be looking mainly at heroes of faith in Ireland and Wales in the fifth and sixth centuries AD.

Each nation is understandably proud of the various saints who lived and ministered in our particular lands, but, for those early saints, their primary loyalty was undoubtedly to the kingdom of God. That loyalty led them to do a lot of travelling and crossing of borders. Their desire was not to protect those borders from hostile armies, but, rather, to engage in spiritual warfare so that those in every land could discover new life in Christ.

Thus, we shall be paying brief visits to the likes of Patrick and Brigid, David and Illtyd. In many cases, we know very little about these saints, but the little snippets of their stories that we do have give us useful insights into the kinds of people they were and how they lived out their faith during those times. Each one we visit will give us a theme to consider and, in this way, they can serve us as guides on our journey with God.

On the last day, we shall think about the countless hosts whose names were never recorded in history, but who, through their faithful witness, contributed just as much as those who became 'famous'. Perhaps these are the ones we warm to most because, for many of us, our journey through life does not take us to fame or, indeed, notoriety. What is often endearing about the stories of these early saints is that they lived close to ordinary men and women in their everyday lives and inspired them to follow Christ. Because we have their stories, these saints from a bygone age can serve us in the same way today.

Michael Mitton

EPHESIANS 6:18–20 (NRSV)

Patrick: pray without ceasing

Pray in the Spirit at all times in every prayer and supplication. To that end keep alert and always persevere in supplication for all the saints. Pray also for me, so that when I speak, a message may be given to me to make known with boldness the mystery of the gospel, for which I am an ambassador in chains. Pray that I may declare it boldly, as I must speak.

Patrick was born around AD390, probably in the north-west of Britain. When he was about 16, a group of raiders captured him and sold him to an Irish chieftain as a slave. He worked herding cattle and, later, in his *Confessio*, he wrote that this was a very significant time for him: 'I prayed frequently through the day; the love of God and the fear of Him increased more and more… for the spirit was fervent within me.' Patrick found an extraordinary gift of turning a crisis into an opportunity. This giving of himself to prayer in such a bleak situation led him on to a path of becoming one of the world's greatest evangelists. He did escape the slavery in Ireland, but God then called him back, not this time as a slave but as a missionary and church-planter.

Patrick would have had much in common with Paul, who also knew what it was to be taken prisoner. As we see in today's passage, although he is in chains, Paul is free in his spirit and encourages the young Christians around him to pray at all times with all kinds of praying.

Both Patrick and Paul knew many tough experiences in their lives and could have been forgiven for sinking into despair, but what keeps them afloat is their praying—inviting the Spirit to lift them to see a different perspective on life and the circumstances in which they found themselves. When pressures come down on us and we feel imprisoned by different life situations, it is good to remember these two pioneers of faith and follow their example to pray in the Spirit.

Prayer

Lord, teach me to 'pray in the Spirit at all times in every prayer and supplication' (v. 18).

MICHAEL MITTON

Brigid: a fiery light

Then you shall call, and the Lord will answer; you shall cry for help, and he will say, Here I am. If you remove the yoke from among you, the pointing of the finger, the speaking of evil, if you offer your food to the hungry and satisfy the needs of the afflicted, then your light shall rise in the darkness and your gloom be like the noonday.

Brigid was born around AD454 and is widely recognised as one of the greatest leaders of the early church in Ireland.

It is said that she was baptised by Patrick and became the abbess of the monastery at Kildare, a community that included men and women. This became a centre for education, culture, worship and hospitality in Ireland.

Brigid came from a wealthy family, but, from an early age, she showed much concern for people in need and annoyed her father by constantly giving away goods and food to the poor! When she became a nun and founded her community at Kildare, it was noted for being a community full of light and compassion. There are many stories of her assisting the poor and freeing slaves. The buildings of her community have long gone, but visitors to the site today will find the cathedral and an eleventh-century round tower, as well as the foundations of the 'fire temple'. It is said that Brigid lit a fire there that only women could keep alight, which they did for a thousand years until the dissolution of the monasteries.

Brigid is a wonderful example of a strong Christian leader who led by example and established a Christian community that testified to the love and grace of God. She would have loved today's passage from Isaiah, which makes clear that if you want to light up a world that is too often shadowed in darkness, then the best thing you can do is to reach out in care for the oppressed and hurting. Equally, if we are personally going through a dark time, the way to find light may be to reach out in compassion to others.

Reflection

What could you do today to bring the light of Christ's compassion to others?

MICHAEL MITTON

Illtyd: wielding the sword of God

Indeed, the word of God is living and active, sharper than any two-edged sword, piercing until it divides soul from spirit, joints from marrow; it is able to judge the thoughts and intentions of the heart. And before him no creature is hidden, but all are naked and laid bare to the eyes of the one to whom we must render an account. Since, then, we have a great high priest who has passed through the heavens, Jesus, the Son of God, let us hold fast to our confession.

Illtyd was probably born of British parents in Brittany in the first half of the fifth century. He was by all accounts highly intelligent and excelled in rhetoric, maths and philosophy.

In his early life, however, Illtyd preferred fighting to studying and legend has it that he was one of King Arthur's knights. On one occasion, he took a group of soldiers hunting in a forest and came across a hermit called Cadoc. Illtyd was immediately impressed by Cadoc and, after spending the day with him, he had a dream that night in which an angel came to him and called him to 'be knight in the service of the King of kings'. Thus, he left his soldiering and became a hermit to fight the spiritual battle. He then founded monasteries, the most famous being the one at Llantwit Major in south Wales, where he used his brilliant mind to teach the people.

Illtyd would have liked today's passage from Hebrews. He had wielded a sword in his time and knew its effects, how it could be used for destructive purposes. Then, all changed after his meeting with Cadoc. He gave himself to studying the word of God and discovered it had extraordinary sharpness and accuracy when it came to matters of the human heart. It was a sword that could make any human feel naked and vulnerable, but this vulnerability does not lead to our destruction because we are in the company of the great high priest.

There are times in life when we need to be stopped in our tracks by the word of God, which may come to us in scripture or through someone like Cadoc, whom we meet in our travels.

Prayer
Lord, let my heart be touched today by your sword of truth.

MICHAEL MITTON

Mark 1:35–39 (NRSV)

Samson of Dol: prayer and action

In the morning, while it was still very dark, [Jesus] got up and went out to a deserted place, and there he prayed. And Simon and his companions hunted for him. When they found him, they said to him, 'Everyone is searching for you.' He answered, 'Let us go on to the neighbouring towns, so that I may proclaim the message there also; for that is what I came out to do.' And he went throughout Galilee, proclaiming the message in their synagogues and casting out demons.

In the sixth century, a sea route much travelled by Christian missionaries ran between South Wales and Brittany, often passing by Devon and Cornwall. Samson was one of the travellers who made use of this route.

Born around AD490, he was educated at Illtyd's monastery at Llantwit, Glamorgan in Wales, and then spent several years along the coast at the community on Caldey Island before living some years as a hermit on the River Severn. It is said that he was escaping the crowds who flocked to see him because of his holiness and miracles, but he had to leave his hermit life when he was made a bishop and became an early episcopal evangelist and church-planter. He worked in Cornwall and the Scilly Isles, where one of the islands is named after him, and crossed over to Brittany, where he established a monastery at Dol. Here, far from being detached from the world, he became involved in the local politics, including organising the excommunication of King Conomor.

Samson is a powerful example of those early Celtic saints who managed to hold together times of withdrawal, prayer and solitude alongside times of high activity, travel and involvement in local communities. They saw themselves as called by God to transform the world in which they lived by means of prayer and action. Today's passage shows this pattern very clearly in the life of Jesus. We all need to be alert to the voice of God, who may call us at one time to withdraw and pray and another to step out in action in his world.

Reflection

How does the balance of withdrawal and involvement seem to be in your own life and ministry?

Michael Mitton

Melangell: the power of a holy life

David said to Abigail, 'Blessed be the Lord, the God of Israel, who sent you to meet me today! Blessed be your good sense, and blessed be you, who have kept me today from blood-guilt and from avenging myself by my own hand! For as surely as the Lord the God of Israel lives, who has restrained me from hurting you, unless you had hurried and come to meet me, truly by morning there would not have been left to Nabal as much as one male.'

Not far from the English border in North Wales lies the Tanat Valley, at the head of which is a small and ancient church dedicated to Melangell.

Melangell was the daughter of an Irish king and, around AD600, she fled from an arranged marriage and lived as a hermit in this remote place. One day, a local prince called Brochwel was nearby, hunting a hare with his dogs. He turned a corner and found the hare being protected by Melangell. She was praying and his dogs refused to disturb her. Brochwel was so impressed by Melangell's piety that he gave her the valley, which in time became the centre for a small community.

There are a number of stories like this in early Celtic Christian history, in which a male aggressor is stopped in his tracks by the power of holiness and prayer embodied by a woman. In Melangell, we see someone who is utterly at peace with herself and her world. She meets aggression not with more aggression but with stillness, and you get the impression that her witness is strong enough to change even a culture steeped in violence and warfare.

Melangell reminds me of Abigail in today's passage. Her husband, Nabal, was a wicked and selfish man. He provoked David, who went to attack him, but Abigail's quick wisdom and generosity not only saved her entire family from death but also prevented David from unnecessary aggression.

There are times when God calls us to meet aggression with prayer, stillness and wisdom. It can take more courage than responding violently, yet it has the power to change a culture.

Reflection
How do you find yourself responding to aggression?

MICHAEL MITTON

David: 'Do ye the little things in life'

And the twelve called together the whole community of the disciples and said, 'It is not right that we should neglect the word of
God in order to wait at tables. Therefore, friends, select from
among yourselves seven men of good standing, full of the Spirit
and of wisdom, whom we may appoint to this task, while we, for
our part, will devote ourselves to prayer and to serving the word.'
What they said pleased the whole community, and they chose
Stephen, a man full of faith and the Holy Spirit.

Visitors to St David's Cathedral on the south-west tip of Wales can see
the restored shrine of David, the mighty Welsh evangelist who died
around AD589.

During David's life, he planted several monasteries in Wales and the
Midlands, but the main community was in the area around the present
cathedral. David taught his monks not only to pray and study but also
to engage in manual labour. The location of his community—near the
coast on a busy sea route—meant that there were many visitors, and
scores of mission ventures set off from this base.

David lived to a great age and apparently his last words were, 'Be
joyful and keep your faith, and do the little things you have seen me
do.' Even today, the phrase 'Do ye the little things in life' is a well-
known phrase in both Welsh and English.

By all accounts, David was an impressive leader, with his good mind
and godly life, and there were several reports of miracles being per-
formed by him. The communities he planted became strong witnesses
for Christ and centres of learning and hard work, but it is interesting to
note that what he really wanted people to remember him for were the
'little things'. For him, the work of the kingdom depended on God's
people being devoted to the apparently insignificant and menial tasks.
It makes me think of Stephen. He agreed to do the practical task of
waiting at tables, but, if you read on in the chapter, you will discover
that, with such a servant-heart, he was used remarkably by God.

Prayer
Lord, help me to do the little things well.

MICHAEL MITTON

Non: prayerfully make things happen

In those days Mary set out and went with haste to a Judean town in the hill country, where she entered the house of Zechariah and greeted Elizabeth. When Elizabeth heard Mary's greeting, the child leapt in her womb. And Elizabeth was filled with the Holy Spirit and exclaimed with a loud cry, 'Blessed are you among women, and blessed is the fruit of your womb. And why has this happened to me, that the mother of my Lord comes to me? For as soon as I heard the sound of your greeting, the child in my womb leapt for joy.'

If you walk from St David's towards the coast, you come to a chapel dedicated to Non, who was the mother of David. That chapel is relatively modern, but, in the field nearby, you can see the ruin of an ancient chapel, also dedicated to Non. Between the two, there is a well. According to tradition, David was born in a thunderstorm and, at the moment of his birth, waters gushed out from the hillside and have been flowing in Non's Well ever since. The story goes that Non, in due course, became a nun, ministering in Cornwall and Brittany, where she died.

Non is one of those Celtic saints about whom not a great deal is known. It is probable that if she had not given birth to David, we would have never heard of her. Yet, her contribution to the work of the gospel in Wales and beyond is considerable, not least because of the way she nurtured her son.

Non might well have felt an affinity with Elizabeth in today's passage. Both Elizabeth and Non carried children who would proclaim the good news. Much as both these mothers loved their sons, what would have thrilled them most was the news their sons proclaimed—that God loved this world so much, he sent Jesus.

Non and Elizabeth represent those who prayerfully make things happen for the cause of the gospel. Their heroism is often unsung, but they are the sort of people who do not mind that!

Reflection

What could you prayerfully make happen for the gospel today?

Michael Mitton

Brynach: love your enemies

[Jesus said] 'But I say to you that listen, Love your enemies, do good to those who hate you, bless those who curse you, pray for those who abuse you. If anyone strikes you on the cheek, offer the other also; and from anyone who takes away your coat do not withhold even your shirt. Give to everyone who begs from you; and if anyone takes away your goods, do not ask for them again. Do to others as you would have them do to you.'

Brynach was born in Ireland some time in the sixth century and may have been of Jewish origin. He developed a strong calling to establish a Christian community in Wales, but he faced a serious problem: he wanted to do so at a time when the Welsh had a deep hatred of the Irish. He made several attempts to settle in Wales at a time when Irish people were being expelled from that part of the world. He was attacked and, on one occasion, seriously wounded, but was cared for by friends who prayed for his healing. Finally, Brynach was granted some land at Nevern and there is still an ancient church there today bearing his name.

There is something truly heroic about Brynach. Undeterred by the hatred of the people, he was determined to plant a Christian community in a land that was deeply hostile to those like him. It may have been precisely because of that hostility that he sought to settle in this part of Wales. He may have seen that if he could found a community there, it would give people an opportunity to change their opinions as a result of forming friendships with an Irish person.

We live in a world torn apart by hatred of people simply because of their race, religion or nationality. Consistently we see, in the course of history, that the one way to heal such divides is for courageous individuals to dare to enter the 'enemy camp' and form friendships. Brynach inspires us to take seriously Jesus' words in today's passage.

Prayer
Father, make me alert to friendships I could form that could heal human divisions.

MICHAEL MITTON

Columba: the power of redemption

Create in me a clean heart, O God, and put a new and right spirit within me. Do not cast me away from your presence, and do not take your holy spirit from me. Restore to me the joy of your salvation, and sustain in me a willing spirit. Then I will teach transgressors your ways, and sinners will return to you. Deliver me from bloodshed, O God, O God of my salvation, and my tongue will sing aloud of your deliverance.

Columba was born a prince, probably in County Donegal in AD521, and could have been the High King of Ireland if he had not decided to become a monk.

Columba planted up to 300 Christian communities in Ireland. He was also a poet and a man of deep feelings, with a strong love for creation. At one time, those deep feelings got the better of him for, in AD561, he got involved in a fierce battle. A synod was called to discuss the battle and, as punishment, Columba was exiled from his beloved Ireland. He sailed to the island of Iona. Although he was distraught at his own sin and having to leave his homeland, he did not dwell on his failings and, instead, built a new community on the island. It was not long before Iona became one of the greatest Christian communities that ever existed and Columba proved to be a brilliant leader of it.

Being suddenly hit by disaster is perhaps one of the hardest experiences in life, particularly when that disaster is of our own making. King David knew this so well, as we see in 2 Samuel 11, which tells the story of David and Bathsheba. Everything was going so well in his reign and his walk with God, but then he committed both adultery and murder. Psalm 51 is his penitent response.

Both David and Columba knew how to come back to God when they had made terrible mistakes. It is clear that God not only pardoned them but also redeemed the mess they had made. Such stories are of great comfort to us fallible humans!

Prayer

Create in me a clean heart, O God, and put a new and right spirit within me.

MICHAEL MITTON

Columbanus: divine restlessness

Now the Lord said to Abram, 'Go from your country and your kin-dred and your father's house to the land that I will show you. I will make of you a great nation, and I will bless you, and make your name great, so that you will be a blessing. I will bless those who bless you, and the one who curses you I will curse; and in you all the families of the earth shall be blessed.' So Abram went, as the Lord had told him; and Lot went with him. Abram was seventy-five years old when he departed from Haran.

Columbanus was born in Leinster, Ireland in AD540. When he was a young man, a woman hermit prophesied that he would become a monk and he settled in the community at Bangor until he was around 50.

One day, he heard the call of God to missionary life and headed to Scotland, England, and then France with a group of twelve other monks, choosing 'voluntary exile for Christ'. For 20 years, he planted several communities in France until, after falling out with the King of Burgundy over his refusal to bless the king's immoral lifestyle, it was necessary to move on again. So, at the age of 70 he moved to Switzer-land, where he stayed for a time near Lake Constance. However, he got into trouble here too, when he opposed some occult groups and felled the trees that had been their idols. He fled over the Alps and, after a short stay in Milan, he settled with his mission team in Bobbio, where he died in his mid-70s. The second part of Columbanus' life was sel-dom without incident and adventure.

Columbanus' story is reminiscent of Abraham's, who, also in the second part of his life, felt a sudden call to move out with God into new territory and engage in a whole new adventure. Like Columbanus, Abraham hit a number of problems and obstacles along the way, but his heart was set on obeying God and following his call. At any moment in life we can become aware of a kind of divine restlessness. We may think life is settled, but God may have other plans!

Reflection

Do you need to listen to a divine restlessness in your soul?

MICHAEL MITTON

ACTS 19:1, 21–22 (NRSV)

Ciaran: at the heart of human affairs

While Apollos was in Corinth, Paul passed through the inland regions and came to Ephesus, where he found some disciples... Now after these things had been accomplished, Paul resolved in the Spirit to go through Macedonia and Achaia, and then to go on to Jerusalem. He said, 'After I have gone there, I must also see Rome.' So he sent two of his helpers, Timothy and Erastus, to Macedonia, while he himself stayed for some time longer in Asia.

Clonmacnoise is one of the most popular pilgrimage places in Ireland. It is in the Irish midlands, on the River Shannon, and visitors find there a wonderful array of ancient buildings, round towers and high crosses. One of the part-ruined buildings is the chapel of Ciaran, who was the founder of this community and known not only for his brilliant mind but also for his miracles and his passion for the poor.

Born in AD516, he was a very bright pupil at the monastery of Clonard, then spent further time training at the monastery of Inishmore on the island of Aran, where he received a vision for the founding of a great monastic community. This vision led to his establishing the community and abbey at Clonmacnoise in AD544. He chose that spot because it was at the crossroads where the busy traffic of the River Shannon met the land traffic of the road that ran west to east across Ireland. So, his community was planted in the busiest place imaginable!

Only seven months after arriving at Clonmacnoise, Ciaran died from the plague. He did not live to see his community become a centre for study, art and literature.

Clonmacnoise is an example of a Christian community being planted at the heart of human affairs. Paul would have had much sympathy with this approach. Indeed, today's passage is part of Paul's third missionary journey, where he planted churches in the major cities of Ephesus and Corinth and planned to go to Rome, the heart of the Empire. Sometimes God calls us to the edges; at other times he calls us to the centre. Like Ciaran and Paul, our job is to be open to God's leading.

Reflection
Where is God calling you to be a witness today?

MICHAEL MITTON

Kevin: listening on the dark side

Then the Lord answered Job out of the whirlwind: 'Who is this that darkens counsel by words without knowledge? Gird up your loins like a man, I will question you, and you shall declare to me. Where were you when I laid the foundation of the earth? Tell me, if you have understanding. Who determined its measurements—surely you know! Or who stretched the line upon it? On what were its bases sunk, or who laid its cornerstone when the morning stars sang together and all the heavenly beings shouted for joy?'

Not far to the south of Dublin, there is a beautiful valley called Glendalough. It was here, towards the end of the sixth century, that a young, thoughtful monk journeyed. His name was Kevin and he had joined a monastery at the age of twelve. When he saw the lower valley at Glendalough, he knew it was the ideal place to plant a community that would, in time, become a thriving centre, including chapel, domestic accommodation, workshops, rooms for writing manuscripts, guest houses, an infirmary and farm buildings. Visitors today can see the remains of later buildings, as this remained a community for many centuries.

Kevin was a deeply sensitive man and a poet, writing a 'Rule for monks' in verse. Increasingly, he felt called to live separately from the main community and moved to be on his own by the upper lake. He chose to live on the dark and shadowed side of the valley, perhaps because he wanted to live as a light in a world darkened by suffering.

Kevin recognised a strong current of creative life in his own soul, which was nurtured by being quiet and spending time experiencing God's creation. Kevin would have admired the book of Job. Job was also one who dwelt in a dark place and knew all about suffering, but from that dark place he had a vision of God which has inspired people for thousands of years. Both Job and Kevin were prepared to be patient in the place of shadows and uncertainty, to wait for God's revelation.

Prayer

Lord, when I find myself dwelling in the valley of shadows, grant me the patience to await your revelation.

MICHAEL MITTON

Brendan: the Spirit in creation

In the beginning God created the heaven and the earth. And the earth was without form, and void; and darkness was upon the face of the deep. And the Spirit of God moved upon the face of the waters. And God said, Let there be light: and there was light. And God saw the light, that it was good: and God divided the light from the darkness. And God called the light Day, and the darkness he called Night.

The story of Brendan's voyage across the Atlantic in a small boat is the most popular tale in all Celtic literature. No doubt, as time went on, the story was much embellished, but there is little doubt that Brendan, the Abbot of Clonfert monastery, who lived through most of the sixth century, did at one time build a boat, boarded it with several other monks and set out in a westerly direction to discover what lay beyond. His intention was to discover the 'Island of Promise'—a quest to discover Paradise. Though there may well have been a literal intention to do this, the voyage of Brendan also has a strong spiritual dimension. It represents a questing for the deeper things of God and his revelation to humans.

Brendan, like Kevin and many others, had a profound respect for creation and, though they believed it had been darkened and harmed by sin and evil, they found it to be a ready instrument in God's hands. It is clear that Brendan and his shipmates delighted in aspects of God's creation, such as icebergs, that seemed miraculous to them. They saw a close connection between the activity of God's Holy Spirit and creation, so would have loved the creation accounts in Genesis, where the Holy Spirit is in evidence, brooding over the water, ready to bring new life.

If you are seeking a new touch of God's Spirit, it may be that you, too, need to spend time outside, enjoying God's created order and being open to the activity of the Spirit.

Prayer
Lord, when I spend time in your beautiful though damaged creation, let me be open to the Spirit of God moving on the waters of my soul.

MICHAEL MITTON

Unknown saints: everyday witness

Greet Apelles, who is approved in Christ. Greet those who belong to the family of Aristobulus. Greet my relative Herodion. Greet those in the Lord who belong to the family of Narcissus. Greet those workers in the Lord, Tryphaena and Tryphosa. Greet the beloved Persis, who has worked hard in the Lord. Greet Rufus, chosen in the Lord; and greet his mother—a mother to me also. Greet Asyncritus, Phlegon, Hermes, Patrobas, Hermas, and the brothers and sisters who are with them.

Any study of the early church in Ireland and Britain will focus on the individuals who have been remembered because they were notable leaders or contributed in a way that caught people's attention. In the last two weeks we have learned something about them from the snippets of writings that have survived. Alongside them, however, are innumerable others whose names never get a mention in the annals of history. What about those heroic monks who joined Brendan in his boat or the women who kept Brigid's fire alight for a thousand years? What about the people whom David, Columba and others put in charge of the mission communities they planted, who had to exercise demanding leadership roles in their infant churches? The success of the early church depended on those whose names we shall never know.

The same could be said for Bible stories: we know a few names, but there are numerous other people who made an enormous difference to the world through their witness but were never noticed. We are given a small window into this 'cloud of witnesses' in Romans 16, however, where Paul names many people who have clearly played a significant role in the building of the kingdom of God. Today, when we remember the saints of our nations, perhaps we should especially give thanks for all the saints, not just the ones who hit the headlines. We should remember, too, that most of us will not achieve prominence, yet still have a vital part to play in the kingdom.

Prayer

Lord, thank you for the host of saints, known and unknown, who have shared the faith in my land. Use me as one such saint today.

MICHAEL MITTON

Suffering, death and hope

'Humankind cannot bear very much reality.' This line from T.S. Eliot's poem *Burnt Norton* can describe our attitude to suffering and death. Fearing both, many people glorify, sanitise or hide away from these aspects of life. Consider the array of euphemisms we have for death: 'passed away', 'departed', 'kicked the bucket', 'gone to a better place'. It feels almost wrong to talk about someone being dead or having died. Worse still, in films, the military and secret services never seem to talk about a real person having been killed. Instead 'the target is down'.

In a society where individuals are expected to cope alone or fall apart, personal suffering such as illness or bereavement is either hidden from view or exposed in the media. Unkind acts or betrayal by those we considered close friends or even family can cause anguish. Corporate greed, pride and fear result in famine, war, poverty and persecution. Environmental tragedies or bacterial or viral epidemics are in significant part caused by our lack of care for God's creation. After a while, however, life for most people returns to 'normal' and it is easy to dismiss or ignore experiences of the rest of humanity.

While humankind might struggle with reality, Christian faith neither glorifies nor trivialises suffering. Instead, God is alongside people as they face difficulties and death, and this is beautifully expressed in the Psalms. Christians worship the God who brings hope in the real world. God experienced suffering and death through Jesus' agony in Gethsemane and on the cross. Jesus' resurrection from the dead and the subsequent coming of the Holy Spirit remind Christians that suffering will come to an end and we shall enjoy an eternity of joy and peace in God's presence. Faith and hope are key elements in a Christian approach to suffering and death, allowing us to bear more reality and accept Jesus' offer of life in all its fullness (John 10:10).

The passages that follow explore ideas of suffering, death and hope. Remembering the 'Great War' and subsequent conflicts, we begin with heroes of faith. Then, over the coming days, we can face the reality of suffering and death, knowing that the hope of Advent is just around the corner.

Lakshmi Jeffreys

Heroes of faith

Now faith is confidence in what we hope for and assurance about what we do not see. By faith Isaac blessed Jacob and Esau... By faith Jacob... blessed each of Joseph's sons... By faith Joseph... spoke about the exodus of the Israelites from Egypt... Moses' parents hid him for three months after he was born, because they saw he was no ordinary child... By faith the people passed through the Red Sea as on dry land... And what more shall I say? I do not have time to tell about Gideon, Barak, Samson and Jephthah, about David and Samuel and the prophets.

The individuals in today's reading include a coward, an adulterer, a boy given away by his parents when he was a baby, a bully, a high-ranking official solely responsible for the death of his only daughter and a political leader who could not take responsibility for making decisions. These rather unlikely heroes are commended to us as people who lived by faith.

Faith in God is being sure of what we hope for with and in God—and being certain of what we do not see, because we know God is in charge. Faith is putting belief into practice. If we believe God is God and God is good, then we live as if that is true. The people in the passage did this in various ways.

Faith always involves some degree of sacrifice and suffering: read the stories of any of the characters in the list. However, faith in God also means that we are not stuck in despair, bitterness, revenge or hopelessness. Hope in God remaining God and good allows us to maintain a proper perspective and face difficulties—even death.

This year marks the centenary of the outbreak of World War I. Today, lists of names will be read out of those who suffered and gave their lives in battle. Like the heroes in our passage, they will have had their personal struggles and failings, but many—then and since—have died in the hope of a better world. In Jesus, we see the ultimate hope for a better world—the ways of the kingdom of God.

Prayer

Lord God, whatever our circumstances, may we live as heroes of faith.

LAKSHMI JEFFREYS

An approach to real life

The Lord is my shepherd, I lack nothing. He makes me lie down in green pastures, he leads me beside quiet waters, he refreshes my soul. He guides me along the right paths for his name's sake. Even though I walk through the darkest valley, I will fear no evil, for you are with me; your rod and your staff, they comfort me. You prepare a table before me in the presence of my enemies. You anoint my head with oil; my cup overflows. Surely your goodness and love will follow me all the days of my life, and I will dwell in the house of the Lord for ever.

David began life as a shepherd, leading and caring for his father's sheep. He ended life as a king, leading and caring for God's people. In both roles, he knew the leading, care and love of God, his shepherd. David experienced God's provision and protection, but he was never immune to danger and suffering. He walked through the darkest valleys, fearing no evil because God was with him. He had enemies—people who sought to end his life—but he still knew God's provision.

What strikes me most is the result of David's experience: 'Surely your goodness and love will follow me all the days of my life' (v. 6). David encountered evil, darkness, enemies and his own sinfulness. Even so, he is not overcome by any of them. Instead, as a result of relying on God's constant presence, when David has been around, God's goodness and love follow after him, perhaps touching the lives of others, too.

I have frequently used this psalm when conducting funerals. It brings comfort as we are reminded that God is with us in suffering, life and death. More than this, it challenges us to consider what remains when we have gone. David walked with God in all circumstances. Despite his struggles (and they were many), he could trust that what would be left after he was gone would be signs of God's goodness, mercy and love.

Reflection

The wake of a ship shows where the ship has been, long after the vessel has disappeared. What is in your wake?

Lakshmi Jeffreys

Who sinned?

As [Jesus] walked along, he saw a man blind from birth. His disciples asked him, 'Rabbi, who sinned, this man or his parents, that he was born blind?' Jesus answered, 'Neither this man nor his parents sinned; he was born blind so that God's works might be revealed in him…' When he had said this, he spat on the ground and made mud with the saliva and spread the mud on the man's eyes, saying to him, 'Go, wash in the pool of Siloam' (which means Sent). Then he went and washed and came back able to see.

In Jesus' time there was thought to be a link between suffering and sin—that is, ignoring or disobeying God. The history of God's people showed them constantly forgetting God's laws and being overcome or even exiled by enemies. Jesus' disciples applied the theory to this man: it must be someone's fault that he had been born blind, they thought.

Even today it is tempting to look for cause and effect. We can understand a heavy smoker developing cancer, but it feels wrong if someone who has neither smoked nor frequented smoky environments gets the disease. We feel that suffering demands someone or something to blame.

Jesus' response was significant. He utterly denied a specific connection between sin and the man's blindness. It was no one's 'fault', he said. Instead, God would use the man's condition to demonstrate what God is really like. Jesus put some mud on the man's eyes and, after the man washed according to Jesus' instructions, his sight was restored.

The name of the pool—'Sent'—is deemed important, emphasising that Jesus was sent by God. However, it is possible that Siloam is the place where a tower fell, killing 18 innocent people (Luke 13:1–4). Here again, Jesus refuted any links between suffering and sin, but stressed the importance of repentance to avoid sin and suffering. I wonder if, after the blind man's encounter with him, Siloam became famous not for the disaster but for this miraculous healing. God's works are shown not simply in the alleviation of suffering but also in the redemption of place, offering hope when there was once sadness and despair.

Prayer

Pray that acts of God will bring hope to places associated with suffering.

LAKSHMI JEFFREYS

I told you so

Then the Lord said to me: Out of the north disaster shall break out on all the inhabitants of the land. For now I am calling all the tribes of the kingdoms of the north, says the Lord; and they shall come and all of them shall set their thrones at the entrance of the gates of Jerusalem, against all its surrounding walls and against all the cities of Judah. And I will utter my judgments against them, for all their wickedness in forsaking me; they have made offerings to other gods, and worshipped the works of their own hands.

Imagine Jeremiah growing up and wondering what he might be in later life: 'one who speaks God's words about the destruction of nations' would not necessarily have made the list!

Jeremiah's message from God would not be a pleasant one to hear and would be even worse to experience. Disaster was coming to God's people from God's hand via enemy states as a sign of judgement. When God's people constantly ignored him, his judgement usually came in the form of allowing them to reap the fruit of their deeds without divine protection. If they chose to trust other nations rather than God, he would leave them to the mercy of those other nations. Thankfully, God's call to Jeremiah later includes the element of hope—that he will build and plant for future growth.

In contrast to yesterday's passage, we see here that sometimes people are significantly responsible for their suffering, despite having been warned about the consequences of their actions. One everyday example is, 'If you buy that on your credit card you'll struggle with the repayments.' God's response, however, is not 'I told you so.' He always provides a solution when we turn back to him, whether or not it was initially our fault. Ultimately, God sent his son Jesus to die on a cross and be raised from death so that all of us have a way back to relationship with God and one another. It might take a while for the credit card debt to be paid, but, with God, there is always hope.

Reflection
If God never says, 'I told you so', neither should we, even to ourselves.

LAKSHMI JEFFREYS

I have had enough

[Elijah] went a day's journey into the wilderness, and came and sat down under a solitary broom tree. He asked that he might die: 'It is enough; now, O Lord, take away my life, for I am no better than my ancestors.' Then he lay down under the broom tree and fell asleep. Suddenly an angel touched him and said to him, 'Get up and eat.' He looked, and there at his head was a cake baked on hot stones, and a jar of water. He ate and drank, and lay down again. The angel of the Lord came a second time, touched him, and said, 'Get up and eat, otherwise the journey will be too much for you.' He got up, and ate and drank; then he went in the strength of that food for forty days and forty nights to Horeb the mount of God.

In theory, Elijah should have been ecstatic. As a result of his obedience to God he had disposed of the prophets of Baal and shown the Lord God of Israel to be the only real God. Moreover, the drought that had gripped the land for three years was now over. It is true, Queen Jezebel had vowed to kill Elijah, but, with God's previous faithfulness to him, surely he would have seen that God would remain with him?

In fact, Elijah felt as if he had been deserted. When questioned by God as to why he was at Horeb, he spoke of his zeal for God, but also of how the rest of God's people had abandoned God's ways and now only he was left. Although angels had provided food and water and he had caught up on sleep, he had had enough and was not afraid to say so!

Teresa of Avila, the 16th-century nun and mystic, is reputed to have said to God, 'If this is how you treat your friends, it is no wonder you have so few.' Like Elijah, though, we are never left unaided. Regardless of our feelings, God will meet us and supply our needs for his service—if we recognise his provision.

Reflection

Jesus' experience of being forsaken by God immediately precedes the hope of resurrection.

LAKSHMI JEFFREYS

The anguish of grief

'Will the Lord spurn for ever, and never again be favourable? Has his steadfast love ceased forever? Are his promises at an end for all time? Has God forgotten to be gracious? Has he in anger shut up his compassion?' And I say, 'It is my grief that the right hand of the Most High has changed.' I will call to mind the deeds of the Lord; I will remember your wonders of old. I will meditate on all your work, and muse on your mighty deeds.

Yesterday we saw how Elijah felt abandoned by God even though he had recently seen God's miraculous intervention to subdue his enemies. Today, the psalmist feels abandoned by God because of bereavement.

Psalm 77 movingly expresses the experience of grief—longing, inability to be comforted, weeping, moaning, sleeplessness. No one understands—seemingly, not even God. The psalmist has no feeling of being loved by God now and worries about never knowing God's compassion again. Has God forgotten to be gracious? This is not a case of being in danger, as Elijah had been. Instead, the psalmist has gone through significant loss and God is nowhere to be found.

Grief is characterised by many questions, none of which has an easy answer, but being able to shout out the questions to God allows the psalmist to recognise reality. While the psalmist's world seems to have fallen apart as a result of grief, God has not changed. Looking back over personal experiences might be too much for the psalmist, so, instead the decision is made to remember what God has done in history and thereby recall what God is like. The psalm ends not with resolution of the psalmist's grief, but a reminder that God led his people across the Red Sea through Moses and Aaron.

It is important to express our anger, fear and sadness to God, regardless of whether or not we feel close to God. In Jesus, God remains the one who has been through suffering and death—and resurrection. As we bring this to mind, God may 'change' our grief so that we are more aware of God being with us in our suffering.

Reflection

Jesus is the way, the truth and the life—even in grief.

LAKSHMI JEFFREYS

Lament

As a deer longs for flowing streams, so my soul longs for you, O God. My soul thirsts for God, for the living God. When shall I come and behold the face of God? My tears have been my food day and night, while people say to me continually, 'Where is your God?' These things I remember, as I pour out my soul... Why are you cast down, O my soul, and why are you disquieted within me? Hope in God; for I shall again praise him, my help and my God.

The psalmist offers a vivid picture to express his longing for God: as water restores life to the parched animal, so God will bring life to him. This is followed by a graphic account of weeping and loneliness as the psalmist acknowledges his profound grief and refers to the question those around him are asking: 'Where is your God?' Then comes a recollection of previous rejoicing in worship—an expression of delight and trust in God—before he pledges to hope in God once again. There is constant movement between faith and feelings, trust in God and being overwhelmed by suffering.

In *Lament for a Son* (SPCK, 1997), American philosopher Nicholas Wolterstorff charts his grief at the death of his 25-year-old son in an accident, using Psalm 42 to address the tension in prayer between lament and trust. He writes powerfully about wanting his son to be returned, while also realising that this will never happen; he prays for God to protect his family, only to remember that he prayed the same for his son.

There are no clear answers as to why God allows people to suffer or permits what we consider untimely death. This can cause us to question God's goodness and love, even though our past experience and shared Christian heritage speak of grace and mercy.

This psalm shows us, however, that, even in the throes of grief, tossed to and fro between trust and lament, we can pour out our thoughts and feelings to God and find at least temporary solace.

Prayer

Read through the whole psalm slowly and pause with the words that speak to you most.

LAKSHMI JEFFREYS

Facing death

Then [Jesus] withdrew from [his disciples] about a stone's throw, knelt down, and prayed, 'Father, if you are willing, remove this cup from me; yet, not my will but yours be done.' Then an angel from heaven appeared to him and gave him strength. In his anguish he prayed more earnestly, and his sweat became like great drops of blood falling down on the ground. When he got up from prayer, he came to the disciples and found them sleeping because of grief, and he said to them, 'Why are you sleeping? Get up and pray that you may not come into the time of trial.'

Jesus was fully human, a young man in his 30s: he would not have wanted to die. Knowing the skill of the Romans in torture, no one in their right mind would choose to be crucified, but Jesus knew what he had to do and needed all the support he could muster to enable him to go through the hideous ordeal. With his closest friends a stone's throw away, Jesus prayed to his heavenly Father.

This passage is usually read during Holy Week, as we journey with Jesus from cries of 'Hosanna!' on Palm Sunday to his agonising death on Good Friday. Perhaps our awareness of the context, of what was soon to happen to him, makes this heart-wrenching prayer more poignant. After the temporary adulation of the crowds, he now faced a cruel death, so he needed to trust God more than ever. 'Father, if you are willing, remove this cup from me. Although I have spoken to my friends about my blood of the new covenant, this cup is too much to bear. But, I trust you so not my will but yours be done.' Jesus' request to God was clear: 'If you are willing, please let this not happen—but it is your will, your kingdom, that makes ultimate sense.'

Jesus knew the immediate future was not what he wanted. Perhaps we face terminal illness—our own or that of a loved one. The prospect of suffering and death was not easy for Jesus and it will not be easy for us, but, with Jesus, death is not the end. This is where real faith begins.

Prayer

For all who face death, Lord, in your mercy, hear their prayers.

LAKSHMI JEFFREYS

What is the point?

At three o'clock Jesus cried out with a loud voice, 'Eloi, Eloi, lema sabachthani?' which means, 'My God, my God, why have you forsaken me?'... Then Jesus gave a loud cry and breathed his last. And the curtain of the temple was torn in two, from top to bottom. Now when the centurion, who stood facing him, saw that in this way he breathed his last, he said, 'Truly this man was God's Son!'

Jesus had prayed to be relieved of his mission, but God did not change the plan. Instead, Jesus died, his last recorded words in Mark's Gospel being this cry of abandonment. For the Roman centurions, this was yet another crucifixion—one of dozens, perhaps hundreds, they had witnessed, so they had hardened themselves to death. For the duty centurion that day, however, Jesus' death was different. There was something about the manner of his death that prompted his remarkable statement about Jesus as God's Son.

At the moment of Jesus' death, 'the curtain of the temple was torn in two, from top to bottom'. The early Christians recognised that this was a physical enactment of the destruction of the barrier between people and God. Jesus' ultimate sacrifice meant that there would never need to be another calf, bull or goat sacrificed. People could now enter God's presence with confidence (Hebrews 10:19). Jesus' death was a necessary sacrifice, but even the centurion would not have known this immediately. All he saw was God's Son.

Jesus himself asked 'Why?' on the cross—and received no immediate answer—but, after three days, God raised him from death. If we have experienced the death of someone close, the same question is often asked and is rarely answered in a manner that satisfies. But death could not hold Jesus. So, if, like the centurion, we recognise and trust him as God's Son, the pain of loss and grief will not hold us for ever. The purpose of Jesus' death was to bring us life eternal. With Jesus, right now, we can know hope and peace, even in the presence of death.

Prayer

Lord Jesus, you are the way, the truth and the life. Please show us today what that means in practice.

LAKSHMI JEFFREYS

Suffering betrayal

While he was still speaking, Judas, one of the twelve, arrived; with him was a large crowd with swords and clubs, from the chief priests and the elders of the people. Now the betrayer had given them a sign, saying, 'The one I will kiss is the man; arrest him.' At once he came up to Jesus and said, 'Greetings, Rabbi!' and kissed him. Jesus said to him, 'Friend, do what you are here to do.' Then they came and laid hands on Jesus and arrested him.

The department head was patrolling the offices looking for a junior at 5 pm on a Friday, which almost certainly meant a late session at the office. The senior with whom Joe worked told him to hide quickly. He squatted down behind a filing cabinet and hid. The department head came rushing into Joe's office, saw the senior who had told Joe to hide and asked if she had seen Joe. 'Yes,' she said, 'he appears to be hiding behind the filing cabinet!'

This is a humorous story and I have no doubt that Joe got his revenge. More seriously, betrayal is perhaps the most destructive event any relationship could encounter and demonstrates a heartless disregard for the victim's dignity, shattering trust. Betrayal of a country by a citizen might endanger whole societies. Betrayal of a child by adults who neglect or abuse rather than showing love and care can wreck a whole life. Betrayal of a marriage partner can destroy families.

Judas was one of Jesus' twelve closest followers, which emphasises the magnitude of his betrayal. That he should identify Jesus to his enemies with a kiss—a sign of respect and affection—was callous. His greeting of 'Rabbi' is heavily ironic: it was as if Judas wanted to demonstrate his utter contempt for the one he formerly knew as 'Lord'. Despite this, Jesus referred to Judas as 'friend', recognising their former closeness and, perhaps, as a rebuke, acknowledging Judas' treachery.

Judas' betrayal of Jesus destroyed both their lives, but Jesus was raised from death. He came through his betrayal and will accompany us through whatever experiences of betrayal we face.

Prayer

Lord Jesus, help us to forgive betrayal as you did.

LAKSHMI JEFFREYS

We had hoped...

And [Jesus] said to them, 'What are you discussing with each other while you walk along?'... Cleopas answered him... 'The things about Jesus of Nazareth, who was a prophet mighty in deed and word before God and all the people, and how our chief priests and leaders handed him over to be condemned to death and crucified him. But we had hoped that he was the one to redeem Israel. Yes, and besides all this, it is now the third day since these things took place. Moreover, some women of our group astounded us. They were at the tomb early this morning, and when they did not find his body there, they came back and told us that they had indeed seen a vision of angels who said that he was alive.'

The point here is that everything the disciples had hoped for was based in reality. Jesus was a prophet, mighty in deed and word—but he was also so much more. Jesus was the one to redeem Israel—but not in the way the disciples expected: 'We had hoped, but our hopes were not fulfilled and now we are dejected and leaving Jerusalem.'

Then, as Cleopas and his companion walked with Jesus and listened to him explaining the scriptures, they began to recognise real hope rather than the false hope they had imagined. By the time Jesus broke bread with them, they saw who he was and were able to begin to live out the hope of Jesus' redemption, not only of Israel but also the whole world.

Sometimes we may cherish a hope for many years, holding on to a wrong image of how we can live it out. For example, the person who has a tremendous love for and rapport with children, but is unable to become a parent, might need to release the hope of being a father or mother in order to discover God's way of true fulfilment, based on the reality of his or her life.

Reflection
'Hope deferred makes the heart sick, but a desire fulfilled is the tree of life' (Proverbs 13:12). *How might you walk with Jesus to discover real hope?*

LAKSHMI JEFFREYS

The power of love

Who will separate us from the love of Christ? Will hardship, or distress, or persecution, or famine, or nakedness, or peril, or sword? As it is written, 'For your sake we are being killed all day long; we are accounted as sheep to be slaughtered.' No, in all these things we are more than conquerors through him who loved us. For I am convinced that neither death, nor life, nor angels, nor rulers, nor things present, nor things to come, nor powers, nor height, nor depth, nor anything else in all creation, will be able to separate us from the love of God in Christ Jesus our Lord.

Katy's parents loved her, but had jobs that required frequent relocation until she was at secondary school. They provided materially for Katy and encouraged her in a variety of activities, but were unable to support her practically or emotionally. Often, as she was beginning to feel part of a friendship group, Katy had to leave. She grew up feeling an outsider, emotionally isolated from her parents and physically not knowing where to call 'home'. However, she successfully hid her struggles, appearing to be a high-flier as an adult, gaining rapid promotion at work.

Over time, Katy discovered that a number of her friends were Christians and she joined a church. From the moment she realised Jesus died for her, she knew beyond any doubt that God loved her. By contrast, it took a number of years for her to feel more than tolerated by her church: she had to grieve past hurts and overcome her desperation to achieve. She gradually recognised that absolutely nothing could separate her from the love of God in Christ Jesus, including her hopes, dreams, failures, successes, grief, joy and any form of suffering. Hope stemmed from God's love for her in Jesus, leaving Katy free to take risks and make mistakes, no longer striving to earn acceptance but live life in all its fullness.

Reflection

When we know we are truly and deeply loved by God, we are free to suffer and grieve fully, knowing that Jesus has gone before us and, even in this life, we shall benefit from this cosmic love.

Lakshmi Jeffreys

Future hope

For out of Zion shall go forth instruction, and the word of the Lord from Jerusalem. He shall judge between many peoples, and shall arbitrate between strong nations far away; they shall beat their swords into ploughshares, and their spears into pruning hooks; nation shall not lift up sword against nation, neither shall they learn war any more; but they shall all sit under their own vines and under their own fig trees, and no one shall make them afraid.

Micah had previously warned the people that there would be trouble ahead if they did not trust in God. The past had been messy, the present was uncertain, but Micah's picture of the future was extraordinary. While there would be imminent conflict and destruction if the people did not turn back to God, even if that happened there was hope. A time would come when people would willingly seek God. Even those banished from the Lord's sight would be restored and forgiven. Within this prophecy are some of the most beautiful words written in the Bible.

What are your hopes for the future? Have you an image of how you want things to be? Listening to the news we might long for an end to suffering without any idea of what that might really look like. We can feel as if we are in the position of Micah's people, living with uneasy alliances and unstable truces, making the most of whoever is around, rather than fully trusting God and experiencing his peace.

The key to managing present suffering and holding on to real hope for the future is to know the God who promises to rule for ever and ever. His rule will be without coercion or other bullying. Our God is one who showed power in death on a cross and resurrection from death. Our God is one who is love. We can hope in and through suffering because we know the God who created all things—and he does not leave us alone. Thus, in the power of the Holy Spirit, we can learn to live as people who bring hope and peace to our suffering world.

Prayer
'May we walk in the name of the Lord our God' (Micah 4:5).

LAKSHMI JEFFREYS

The best is yet to come

Then I saw a new heaven and a new earth; for the first heaven and the first earth had passed away, and the sea was no more. And I saw the holy city, the new Jerusalem, coming down out of heaven from God, prepared as a bride adorned for her husband. And I heard a loud voice from the throne saying, 'See, the home of God is among mortals. He will dwell with them; they will be his peoples, and God himself will be with them; he will wipe every tear from their eyes. Death will be no more; mourning and crying and pain will be no more, for the first things have passed away.'

Julian of Norwich was a 13th-century 'anchoress'—a woman who set herself apart for God in life and prayer. She was dying and receiving the last rites when she had 16 revelations of Jesus. After recovering, she wrote about all she had experienced. The 13th of these 'showings' answered one of her dilemmas: why should an all-powerful God allow sin and suffering? Jesus' response was, 'It was necessary that there should be sin; but all shall be well, and all shall be well, and all manner of thing shall be well.'

The scene described in our passage today offers a similar message. We may never understand sin and suffering, but there will be a new heaven and a new earth. God will be as intimate with people as was intended in the beginning. There is powerful tenderness in the image of every tear being wiped away.

The new creation is a picture not only of how life will be, but of how life can be now, albeit incompletely, when we choose to live with God at the centre. Every now and then we are offered glimpses of what is to come, when we shall trust God fully forever. This future hope can encourage us through our present experiences of suffering and death. We can live with God, who has overcome such things and will continue to do so. All shall be well. The best is yet to come.

Prayer
Lord God, may we dwell with you and you with us, now and always.

LAKSHMI JEFFREYS

Gardens and God

Wandering the back streets of a southern Mediterranean or north African city, you may find yourself passing a high stone wall. If you do, look up: you may be rewarded by a glimpse of lush greenery just climbing over the top and perhaps hear the faint sound of falling water coming from a hidden garden. The locked garden squares found in central London also offer tantalising glimpses of escape from city pavements into a realm of verdant lawns and manicured rose beds—but only for those privileged enough to be key-holders.

In so many countries, the secluded, well-tended garden is synonymous with living the good life. It is a place to relax, enjoy yourself and create an atmosphere of beauty and harmony (even if you employ somebody else to do the literal dirty work). In a dry and dusty land, abundance of water and vegetation are particular luxuries and it is hardly surprising that when we turn to the Bible, we find a variety of well-watered gardens described—both actual places and also metaphors for the spiritual state of an individual or people.

Over the next few days, we will consider some of these gardens described in the Bible, ranging from groves of trees outside Jerusalem to Eden, the original garden paradise. It is a helpful reminder that the story of creation is not only about us—men and women, called to 'fill the earth and subdue it' (Genesis 1:28). Before we came along on the sixth day, God had been at work shaping the cosmos, every single bit of which he judged to be 'good'. Just as we are described as being made in God's image (v. 26), so we can learn something of God not only from each other but also by looking at the work of his hands (in accordance with the reasoning known as 'natural theology').

The season of harvest may be past as we come to these readings, but the imperative of thankfulness remains. God has blessed us with a beautiful world and given us the task of making it more beautiful. We can and should thank him for the fertility of the earth that provides not only food for the body but also food for the soul.

Naomi Starkey

GENESIS 2:8–10, 15–17 (NRSV)

Paradise remembered

And the Lord God planted a garden in Eden, in the east; and there he put the man whom he had formed. Out of the ground the Lord God made to grow every tree that is pleasant to the sight and good for food, the tree of life also in the midst of the garden, and the tree of the knowledge of good and evil. A river flows out of Eden to water the garden... The Lord God took the man and put him in the garden of Eden to till it and keep it. And the Lord God commanded the man, 'You may freely eat of every tree of the garden; but of the tree of the knowledge of good and evil you shall not eat, for in the day that you eat of it you shall die.'

When thinking of Eden, it is easy to imagine a kind of stately home splendour—all herbaceous borders and clipped yews, with Adam toiling away alongside his wheelbarrow. If we focus on what the Bible passage actually says, we notice that Eden sounds more like an oasis. God provides a 'garden' of fruiting trees with an abundant water supply; it is up to the man to 'till it and keep it' (v. 15).

Notice that the text uses 'Lord God' (vv. 8, 15), combining the covenant name YHWH, disclosed to Moses, with 'Elohim', the name for God in Genesis 1. Here, God is recognised both as Creator and as covenant partner with the human race. The Creator/covenant-making one, in his care for humanity, does not simply provide a suitable home and profitable work to do but also creates conditions: 'You may freely eat... you shall not eat' (vv. 15, 17).

Why should gaining knowledge about good and evil lead to death? A moment of reflection on the state of the world shows that knowledge exercised without wisdom can lead to immense suffering. We must accept our limitations, our human frailty, and ask for God's help before we can hope to begin to live wisely and use our knowledge well.

Reflection

We cannot begin the journey away from fragmentation towards wholeness until we accept our own and the world's woundedness.

Ray Simpson, *Hilda of Whitby* (BRF, 2014)

NAOMI STARKEY

The garden of love

A garden locked is my sister, my bride, a garden locked, a fountain sealed. Your channel is an orchard of pomegranates with all choicest fruits, henna with nard, nard and saffron, calamus and cinnamon, with all trees of frankincense, myrrh and aloes, with all chief spices—a garden fountain, a well of living water, and flowing streams from Lebanon. Awake, O north wind, and come, O south wind! Blow upon my garden that its fragrance may be wafted abroad. Let my beloved come to his garden, and eat its choicest fruits.

Here is another paradisaical garden, overflowing with sensory—and sensual—delight. The lover is expounding the beauty of his bride, listing a bewildering array of scented plants and fruits to evoke quite how lovely she is. The NRSV notes, delicately, 'meaning of Hebrew uncertain' for the word translated 'channel', so I will leave it to you to ponder what this lover may have been talking about.

As with Eden, this garden has an ample water supply, with a well that constantly bubbles up, fresh and 'living', even though the fountain is 'sealed'. There are further reminders of Eden in the mention of eating 'choice fruits', but, in this garden of bliss, eating these fruits means celebrating love and life, not embarking on a path leading to loss and pain, as did the man and woman in Eden.

This is also a 'garden locked': the woman will release herself only for her lover, who will give himself to her alone (2:16; 6:3; 7:10, although mention of 'Solomon' elsewhere brings to mind the very different and far less balanced relationships between kings and harems). Just as a dam holds back water so that it can be released safely, so, within the boundaries of faithfulness and commitment, deep love and desire can be safely expressed. Within these boundaries, such love can be channelled for nurturing, as well as delighting, another, rather than simply employed to satisfy our own appetites.

Reflection

We need to understand and control our passions, for through them we can recognise and release the divine self-giving love of creation.

Andrew Clitherow, *Desire, Love and the Rule of St Benedict* (SPCK, 2008)

NAOMI STARKEY

Land grab

Naboth the Jezreelite had a vineyard in Jezreel, beside the palace of King Ahab of Samaria. And Ahab said to Naboth, 'Give me your vineyard, so that I may have it for a vegetable garden... I will give you a better vineyard for it; or, if it seems good to you, I will give you its value in money.' But Naboth said to Ahab, 'The Lord forbid that I should give you my ancestral inheritance.' Ahab went home resentful and sullen... He lay down on his bed, turned away his face, and would not eat... As soon as Ahab heard that Naboth was dead, Ahab set out to go down to the vineyard of Naboth the Jezreelite, to take possession of it.

I recall years of driving along the A40 in London, past rows of boarded-up semis purchased for a road-widening scheme that never happened. The gardens of the empty houses ran wild, with only the occasional shrub or tree serving as a reminder of their former owners' care by continuing to bud each spring.

The 'compulsory purchase' in our passage today is a blatant land grab, an extreme example of power abused. Naboth pays with his life for protecting his ancestral piece of ground (v. 13) from the predatory king. The land (the promised land) was God's gift to his people, the foundation of the covenant, along with the Law that showed them how they should live. Land was to be considered as held in trust for the Lord God (Leviticus 25:23) rather than treated as a disposable commodity.

I find it impossible to reflect on this story without being reminded of present-day issues of territory and possession in the Holy Land, a region that we should remember is sacred to Christians, Jews and Muslims. In our response to such a complex and immensely painful situation as we see there today, we should resist the temptation to give quick answers and reflect instead on the wider message of scripture—that we are called to work for justice, peace and care for all.

Reflection

'They shall all sit under their own vines and under their own fig trees, and no one shall make them afraid; for the mouth of the Lord of hosts has spoken' (Micah 4:4).

Naomi Starkey

Fruitless labour

My beloved had a vineyard on a very fertile hill. He dug it and cleared it of stones, and planted it with choice vines; he built a watch-tower in the midst of it, and hewed out a wine vat in it; he expected it to yield grapes, but it yielded wild grapes... And now I will tell you what I will do to my vineyard. I will remove its hedge, and it shall be devoured; I will break down its wall, and it shall be trampled down... and it shall be overgrown with briers and thorns; I will also command the clouds that they rain no rain upon it. For the vineyard of the Lord of hosts is the house of Israel, and the people of Judah are his pleasant planting; he expected justice, but saw bloodshed; righteousness, but heard a cry!

It looked so promising—fertile soil, good situation, choice plants, a hard-working gardener—but the toil, expense and patience did not pay off. Instead of the anticipated abundance, the 'beloved' (an echo of the Song of Songs perhaps) ends up with a useless crop of small, sour fruit. His disappointment and anger are graphically described—and the prophet's punchline comes at the end. What he is speaking about are the nations of Israel and Judah.

What the story reveals is both the extent of God's loving care in tending his 'vineyard' and also the extent of his anger when that care does not yield a harvest. To drive home the point that this is wilful, rather than involuntary, fruitlessness, we have the contrast (involving wordplay in the original Hebrew) of bloodshed instead of justice, a crying out instead of righteousness.

Jesus uses similar imagery in the parable of the tenants (found in Matthew, Mark and Luke) and in John 15:1: 'I am the true vine, and my Father is the vine-grower.' Biblical teaching reflected clearly the life and times of the people to whom it was addressed, drawing illustrations from what was to be seen and experienced all around. If we preach and teach the Bible, it is good to bear this in mind.

Reflection

'Those who abide in me and I in them bear much fruit, because apart from me you can do nothing' (John 15:5).

NAOMI STARKEY

Betrayal in the garden

[Jesus] went out with his disciples across the Kidron valley to a place where there was a garden, which he and his disciples entered. Now Judas, who betrayed him, also knew the place, because Jesus often met there with his disciples. So Judas brought a detachment of soldiers together with police from the chief priests and the Pharisees, and they came there with lanterns and torches and weapons. Then Jesus, knowing all that was to happen to him, came forward and asked them, 'For whom are you looking?' They answered, 'Jesus of Nazareth.' Jesus replied, 'I am he.' Judas, who betrayed him, was standing with them.

I was talking to a travel writer who spoke of how his faith had grown as a result of visiting Israel. Although he already knew, of course, that the events of Jesus' life took place in a real landscape, which can still be visited today, he had not reckoned on the powerful spiritual impact of actually walking in those places.

There are four contenders for the site that John names as the garden where Jesus spent the night before his betrayal (it is only called 'Gethsemane', Aramaic for 'oil press', in the Gospels of Matthew and Mark). Even so, the visitor can get a sense of what the garden would have looked like. A grove of olive trees rather than our preconceived notion of flowers and shrubs, it would still have been a place of pleasant shade where, John tells us, Jesus would 'often' meet with his disciples.

John's Gospel is known for its layers of meaning and the richness of its imagery. We should not feel we are being too fanciful, then, if we detect echoes here of God walking in Eden, with the man and the woman he had made. Back then, as in our passage today, the garden was a place of struggle between good and evil, a place of betrayal, of the darkness seeming to defeat the light.

As we will see tomorrow, though, it is in another of John's gardens that we witness the light triumphing over the darkness, once and for all.

Reflection
'The light shines in the darkness, and the darkness did not overcome it' (John 1:5).

NAOMI STARKEY

Garden burial

> Joseph of Arimathea, who was a disciple of Jesus, though a secret one… asked Pilate to let him take away the body of Jesus… Nicodemus, who had at first come to Jesus by night, also came, bringing a mixture of myrrh and aloes, weighing about a hundred pounds. They took the body of Jesus and wrapped it with the spices in linen cloths, according to the burial custom of the Jews. Now there was a garden in the place where he was crucified, and in the garden there was a new tomb in which no one had ever been laid. And so, because it was the Jewish day of Preparation, and the tomb was nearby, they laid Jesus there.

Although Jesus is buried stealthily, by two secret disciples, it is still a kingly burial. He is accorded the honour of being the first to be laid in a newly made tomb, his body dressed with a huge quantity of spices, presumably as pungent as any evoked in the poetry of the Song of Songs.

The scene is one that, in its very familiarity, can lose its emotional power, but we can reread the passage now, lingering over the twice-repeated phrase 'the body of Jesus'. Two men tend the corpse of one who, when living, healed the sick with no more than a word and raised the dead. Joseph and Nicodemus, reverently folding the battered limbs of their rabbi and friend in linen cloths, would surely have remembered such scenes and struggled to understand, yet again, how things could have come to such a terrible end.

The wonder of this garden is to be revealed in a matter of hours—for it is the place where the miracle of resurrection will have the last word, instead of the despair of death. On Easter morning, Mary Magdalene comes, looks through her tears and mistakes the risen Jesus for the gardener—which, in a way, he is, just like his Father.

Reflection

Now the green blade riseth from the buried grain,
Wheat that in dark earth many days has lain;
Love lives again, that with the dead has been:
Love is come again, like wheat that springeth green.

John Crum (1928)
NAOMI STARKEY

Harvesting the fruits of the garden

The time is surely coming, says the Lord, when the one who
ploughs shall overtake the one who reaps, and the treader of
grapes the one who sows the seed; the mountains shall drip sweet
wine, and all the hills shall flow with it. I will restore the fortunes
of my people Israel, and they shall rebuild the ruined cities and
inhabit them; they shall plant vineyards and drink their wine, and
they shall make gardens and eat their fruit. I will plant them upon
their land, and they shall never again be plucked up out of the
land that I have given them, says the Lord your God.

Ruins rebuilt, a land dripping with wine (it was once described as 'flowing with milk and honey', Exodus 3:8) and so fertile that the harvest is
still being gathered as the new crops are planted. Unlike Isaiah's
'beloved', with his failed vineyard, the people will literally enjoy the
fruits of their labours—and no enemy will steal it from them.

What we see here is not only the promise of restoration after exile,
but an undoing of the consequences of the Fall, when years of sweat
and toil would produce no more than the bare essentials of life, amid a
lot of 'thorns and thistles' (Genesis 3:17–19). Without going as far as
full-on prosperity theology, on the basis of this and many other Bible
passages we can safely say that God wants the best for his people. He
made a good and beautiful world to delight his earth-creatures. When
they rejected relationship and chose their own selfish ways, again and
again and again, they reaped the bitter consequences.

Here, though, the Lord himself declares that he will overturn those
consequences. He wants to set everything to rights, the way it was
meant to be, from the beginning. That is the hope in which we, too,
live. Whatever our failures, our wounds, our self-inflicted catastrophes,
the Lord God is in the business of making good. He will, one day, fix
us, and our lives will bear good fruit.

Reflection

*God never ever tires of forgiving us. It is we who tire of asking
for forgiveness.*

From Pope Francis' first Angelus, St Peter's Square (17 March 2013)

NAOMI STARKEY

Son of God/Son of Man: Jesus in Mark's Gospel

The good news of Jesus Christ, the Son of God (Mark 1:1) is what Christianity is about. If we want to be better Christians, we need to open ourselves to divinity that clothes humanity and be made expert in pointing people to the miracle of Jesus' coming, death and resurrection.

In my work as a parish priest, Mark's Gospel is a prime tool that I give to people whenever I can—especially couples preparing for marriage or the baptism of their children. I hand them Mark because:

- It is the shortest of the Gospels, easily slips in your pocket or handbag, and can be read in little more than an hour and a half.
- It is the earliest of the Gospels, possibly written close to Peter's death, around AD64, which, not discounting the historical authenticity of the others, has special appeal to those who want to get the facts about Jesus.
- It is fast-moving as it contains less teaching than the other Gospels.
- It includes provocative aspects, such as Jesus' call to secrecy about his miracle-working, that make for open-ended conversations.
- Half the Gospel is about Holy Week, so readers are left in no doubt when assessing the life of Jesus that his death and resurrection are key to what he is about.

This Advent Sunday, 30 November, the Roman Catholic, Anglican and other denominations commence Sunday readings for 2014–2015 with Mark's Gospel. So, *New Daylight* readers are invited to get ready, possibly ahead of their churches, over the next fortnight as we look at some highlights of this foundational Christian document.

Mark's Gospel is about who Jesus is, what he did and the impact it has on us. I have chosen 'Son of God/Son of Man' as the title since it expresses a tension in the Gospel related to the understanding of Jesus Christ. The Christian understanding of this tension makes it the wellspring of God's purpose for humanity: the Son of God becoming the Son of Man, so (in the traditional, non-inclusive phrase), 'children of men' become 'children of God'. This is the good news of Jesus Christ, the Son of God, as it works out in our lives.

John Twisleton

MARK 1:9–11 (NRSV)

Be what you are

In those days Jesus came from Nazareth of Galilee and was baptised by John in the Jordan. And just as he was coming up out of
the water, he saw the heavens torn apart and the Spirit descend-
ing like a dove on him. And a voice came from heaven, 'You are
my Son, the Beloved; with you I am well pleased.'

I treasure two occasions when God spoke to me directly of his special
love for me and his purpose for my life. One was my call to the priest-
hood. The second came after my faith had burned low and he answered
my prayer, 'God where are you?', by speaking through a leaf on a tree:
'I made you. I love you. I want to fill you with my Spirit.' It is wonderful
how such rare spiritual encounters can energise our lives through our
thankful remembrance of them.

Jesus had far more to remember thankfully than I have. The evangelist Mark starts his Gospel by relating Jesus' baptism at the hands of
John the Baptist, how he heard aloud that he was God's beloved Son
and was anointed by the Holy Spirit. The implication of this event for
Jesus seems to have been to clarify who he was to himself and set him
off on his three-year course towards Calvary. The other Gospels confirm
that the Holy Spirit was with him from his conception, so we could see
this event as a manifesting of what was already at work in God's Son
who had become also Mary's son.

On this Advent Sunday, let us remember that to be a Christian is to
share in the anointing of the Anointed One. Jesus Christ means 'Jesus
the Anointed' and, as in John's account of his baptism, 'He on whom
you see the Spirit descend and remain is the one who baptises with the
Holy Spirit' (John 1:33). That Holy Spirit's anointing guarantees our
knowledge of who we are—God's beloved daughters and sons—and
gives us the call to be what we are.

Prayer
*Lord, in baptism you made me your child and gave me your Spirit. May I
always treasure both what you made me and what you are making me.
Amen*

JOHN TWISLETON

Living free

> One sabbath [Jesus] was going through the cornfields; and as they made their way his disciples began to pluck heads of grain. The Pharisees said to him, 'Look, why are they doing what is not lawful on the sabbath?'… Then he said to them, 'The sabbath was made for humankind, and not humankind for the sabbath; so the Son of Man is lord even of the sabbath.'

'News is bad for your health. It leads to fear and aggression, and hinders your creativity and ability to think deeply. The solution? Stop consuming it altogether' (Rolf Dobelli, 'News is bad for you', *The Guardian*, 12 April 2013). When I read this, it chimed with my sense that I was living under a wearying regime of attending to news feeds. It led me to break with the habit and decide that, for me personally, it was better to start the day more gently with Classic FM rather than BBC Radio 4's *Today* programme. I still get enough news to pray about, but am no longer in such slavery to it that my spiritual freedom is hampered.

Mark's Gospel alone includes the remarkable challenge of Jesus to the letter of Jewish law—that the sabbath was made for humankind and not humankind for the sabbath—which goes on to exempt himself and his disciples from the letter of that law. It is teaching that would have been of particular encouragement to Mark's readership—non-Palestinian Christians of non-Jewish origin.

To live in the freedom Jesus brings is a work of the Holy Spirit aided by God's commandments. It calls for a higher and creative obedience than the literalistic interpretation of the commandments of his then co-religionists or the similarly slavish patterns of living we get snared up in ourselves. I saw my life was being hampered by my news obsession and this helped me take decisive action to free myself from it.

Jesus is the Son of God and Son of Man. As the divine Son, he brings a reminder of God's highest priorities, but, as the Son of Man, he serves to bring humanity into its right mind by his repeated call for us to repent.

Reflection
Why not ask the Lord to show you any obsessions you need to break?

JOHN TWISLETON

Sovereign freedom

> [Jesus] told his disciples to have a boat ready for him because of the crowd, so that they would not crush him; for he had cured many, so that all who had diseases pressed upon him to touch him. Whenever the unclean spirits saw him, they fell down before him and shouted, 'You are the Son of God!' But he sternly ordered them not to make him known.

Mark's account of Jesus is one of a man with a mission. Healing is part of that mission to this day because Jesus calls and authorises his disciples to both preach and heal.

In this incident at the start of the Gospel, we read that he had cured many, so all who had diseases 'pressed upon him to touch him' (v. 10). This authority of Jesus over sickness and evil spirits is linked to his authority as the Son of God or Messiah who came in fulfilment of Old Testament prophecy. The healings and miracles are a pointer to who Jesus is, as the Son of God who also became the Son of Man.

The recognition of Jesus for who he is occurs throughout the Gospel, alongside refusals to recognise and partial recognitions—starting with Jesus himself at his baptism, Peter's profession midway and the centurion's acknowledgement at the end. Today's passage shows how he is recognised from the start by evil spirits, who, alert to God's coming to earth, shout out the truth of it in a strange and frightening manner.

This section of chapter 3 invites us to reflect on God's sovereignty in terms of both healing and faith. 'All' the people pressed on him but Jesus heals 'many' (v. 10), and this is so today when it comes to physical cures occurring in answer to prayer. Why is it that some are healed and not others? Similarly, why is it that, among our acquaintances, many more would tend to see Jesus as the Son of Man than the Son of God? It is strange that even the demons believe (James 2:19). The answers to these questions lie beyond human thinking, in God's sovereign freedom to act and choose to do as he sees best.

Reflection

God's sovereignty: 'nor are your ways my ways' (Isaiah 55:8).

JOHN TWISLETON

107

Selective deafness

When [Jesus] was alone, those who were around him along with the twelve asked him about the parables. And he said to them, 'To you has been given the secret of the kingdom of God, but for those outside, everything comes in parables; in order that "they may indeed look, but not perceive, and may indeed listen, but not understand; so that they may not turn again and be forgiven."'

There are many passages in the Bible that confound our reason and Mark 4:10–12 is one of them. Elsewhere in the New Testament, the evidence is that Jesus presented himself and his message equally to all. In this passage, we see insider disciples contrasted with those outside. There is also an interpretation of parables using words from Isaiah 6:9 that speaks of them as being concerned to conceal rather than reveal truth. What are we to make of this?

Some scholars see these verses as imported, non-authentic sayings of Jesus. Most wrestle with their sense, although many at least would see their existence as proof that this literature is no fabrication. If the story of Jesus were made up, what would be the point of recording these sorts of contradictions?

As the verses are part of the canon of scripture, they have potential spiritual benefit to readers who approach them in faith. As I have prayed through them, I have come to see them, as in yesterday's reflection, as being linked to God's sovereignty only from the human end. Just as someone who is not totally deaf can be guilty of hearing what they want to hear and ignoring what is unpalatable to them, so it is with hearing God. Parables are given in the sovereignty of God to help and not hinder divine communication, but only those who bow to God as sovereign and deep down want to hear from him get the point.

When it comes to getting to know God, our intellect has to give way to our will, which is so often the agent of repentance and faith.

Prayer
Lord, we bow to your sovereign purpose for our lives and beg you to open our inner ears so we can listen, understand, turn again and be forgiven.
Amen

JOHN TWISLETON

MARK 5:25–29, 34 (NRSV)

Carpe diem (seize the day)

Now there was a woman who had been suffering from haemor-rhages for twelve years. She had endured much under many physicians, and had spent all that she had; and she was no better, but rather grew worse. She had heard about Jesus, and came up behind him in the crowd and touched his cloak, for she said, 'If I but touch his clothes, I will be made well.' Immediately her haem-orrhage stopped; and she felt in her body that she was healed of her disease... [Jesus] said to her, 'Daughter, your faith has made you well.'

I went to the doctor's, only to find one of my church members having a nose bleed, linked to being on blood-thinning medication after a hip replacement. I said a prayer with him before I saw the doctor myself. On my return to the waiting room, he was beaming. He insisted my prayer had stopped the bleeding, so we could all go home! I had seized the moment—*carpe diem*!

In the Gospel account, it was a woman with a terrible blood flow who was the opportunist. She saw that Jesus was in a rush to go and see Jairus' daughter (vv. 22–24), so, not wishing to delay his mercy mission, just touched his clothing. 'If I but touch his clothes, I will be made well,' she thought. The woman had faith and saw Jesus for who he was—the Son of God, all powerful, and Son of Man, all loving. As soon as she touched him, her haemorrhage stopped 'and she felt in her body that she was healed of her disease'.

The miracle came as power flowed from Jesus, but the story ended with Jesus applauding her faith as the equal agent of her healing. She seized the moment, recognising that God was right there in it, waiting for her, and as a result she saw his possibilities realised in her life.

Reflection

Have there been moments recently when you have found God powerfully present in your life? How attentive are you to the Holy Spirit's close presence in every situation? In what measure can you identify with the faith expectancy of the woman with the haemorrhage?

JOHN TWISLETON

Uncomfortable stuff

[Jesus] left that place and came to his home town, and his disciples followed him. On the sabbath he began to teach in the synagogue, and many who heard him were astounded. They said, 'Where did this man get all this?...' And they took offence at him. Then Jesus said to them, 'Prophets are not without honour, except in their home town, and among their own kin, and in their own house.' And he could do no deed of power there, except that he laid his hands on a few sick people and cured them. And he was amazed at their unbelief.

Home comforts can deceive. The people of Nazareth lost out on receiving Jesus because comfort and familiarity with him blinded them to his extraordinary nature. He was their son, so his kin and fellow villagers could not see him as he really was and is—the Son of God.

The more humble title, Son of Man, literally meaning 'man', occurs on the lips of Jesus 42 times in Mark's Gospel. It is used by him to speak of his doings and predict his coming sufferings. It is also, on some occasions, identified with the mysterious figure to come in the clouds, mentioned in Daniel 7:13. Even this more humble self-understanding was controversial.

In the synagogue, many who heard him were astounded, but they still took offence at him. What was controversial in his home town seems to have been less his healings and miracles than the idea that God was at work in and through him. Nazareth chose to remain in disbelief, despite being faced with all the evidence of his divine mission. This rejection from his home town anticipates the final rejection of the Son of Man by his own nation that is recorded later, in the account of his passion.

As Mark records in verse 5–6, God's immeasurable power seems to be frequently held back from working when disbelief is present.

Reflection

Is there hostility to my Christian faith among those near to me? Might this be due to my own failings? Or could it be that they are taking offence against something of Christ in my life?

JOHN TWISLETON

The heart of the matter

[Jesus] said to [his disciples], '... Do you not see that whatever goes into a person from outside cannot defile, since it enters, not the heart but the stomach, and goes out into the sewer?... It is what comes out of a person that defiles. For it is from within, from the human heart, that evil intentions come: fornication, theft, murder, adultery, avarice, wickedness, deceit, licentiousness, envy, slander, pride, folly. All these evil things come from within, and they defile a person.'

As a priest committed to the pattern of daily prayer known as the Daily Office, I am regularly brought up short when I go to the local monastery, because they say the Psalms much more slowly than I do in my private devotions. In sharing their service, I recognise how much I say prayers 'to get through them' rather than to be fully present to God. Left to myself, my prayer easily goes off the rails and becomes self-orientated.

In his earthly ministry, Jesus made a point of challenging self-satisfied religion, as in this incident in Mark 7, after the accusations that his disciples had not washed before dinner as the purity laws required. Mark is handing on the story to Gentile Christians, who, in his day, were engaged in a similar conflict over the degree to which they should take on Jewish practice.

The food going into us does not matter as much as the words and deeds that come out of us. How brilliant a capacity Jesus has for turning things on their head!

Jesus knew our nature through and through. His challenge to ritual law does not extend to the core commandments of God, but gives us a reminder to examine our spiritual practices, lest they get dissociated from the call to obey God and thus become ends in themselves. Even the daily study of Bible reading notes is not exempt!

Reflection

As you read today's notes, your reflection on the scriptures is what matters most. There is no word of God that lacks power—and it can counter the power of sin within you.

JOHN TWISLETON

Sunday 7 December

MARK 8:27–30 (NRSV)

The mystery of faith

> Jesus went on with his disciples to the villages of Caesarea Philippi; and on the way he asked his disciples, 'Who do people say that I am?' And they answered him, 'John the Baptist; and others, Elijah; and still others, one of the prophets.' He asked them, 'But who do you say that I am?' Peter answered him, 'You are the Messiah.' And he sternly ordered them not to tell anyone about him.

Of all the four Gospel writers, Mark gives proportionately more space to the cross. Almost half his Gospel focuses on Holy Week, and Peter's confession of Jesus as Messiah provides the turning point for the following predictions and description of Jesus' sufferings.

By Mark 8, we have become aware of a powerful dynamic of teaching and healing in Jesus. Now, in Peter's confession of faith, we are given an insight into what (or who) lies behind the action. In Matthew's version of this event, Peter's faith is credited as a gift from God. To this day, the ministry of bishops of Rome (which so many Christians believe to have originated in Peter) is a gift welcomed by many and reckoned to guard the essence of Christianity—faith in Christ as the divine Son of God.

Peter's confession is a hinge event that links the Son of God and Son of Man, divine redeemer and suffering servant. We see God in power at first, but only as preparation for us to see God's glory shining out in human weakness.

Is this Gospel really just a passion narrative with an introduction? Perhaps we can read this structure as a parable of our human condition. Like Jesus in the Gospel, we may be active in God's service until the years advance and we need to submit to being 'done to' rather than being 'doers'. Our Lord is the same yesterday, today and for ever, so Mark's account of his actions and passion can be, for us, an eternal source of comfort.

Reflection

Are there circumstances I bear that are beyond my control? Can I see these hardships as being carried with Jesus in his passion and so invested with his redemptive power? How can Mark's focus on the cross speak into my life today?

JOHN TWISLETON

Why Jesus came

> They went on from there and passed through Galilee. [Jesus] did not want anyone to know it; for he was teaching his disciples, saying to them, 'The Son of Man is to be betrayed into human hands, and they will kill him, and three days after being killed, he will rise again.' But they did not understand what he was saying and were afraid to ask him.

Mark's Gospel is about the good news of Jesus Christ, the Son of God (Mark 1:1). That good news has been revealed in historical events, of which this Gospel is a privileged witness as the earliest story of Jesus' life. The foretelling in today's passage of his repudiation, death and rising is one of three that Jesus gives in Mark's account.

How historically sound are these predictions? Do they not have a similar feel to those written by Paul in earlier Christian documents, such as 1 Corinthians 15:3–4? Might they have been put on Jesus' lips by the writer, in the light of the resurrection? There is no 'knock down' answer to legitimate questions such as these because the Gospel writers were writing of someone alleged to have risen from the dead, and they could not but view the memories of Jesus' incarnate life in that stupendous light. Jesus' speaking of himself as the Son of Man, however, is hardly contested by scholars, nor is the particular reinterpretation he gave of that biblical title as one who suffers in fulfilment of scripture.

If these predictions were invented by Mark, they would have required more creativity than if they were based on what Jesus actually said. If Mark was inventing or tidying up rather than faithfully chronicling the life of Jesus, would he have included the repeated emphasis on secrecy about what was happening or on the misunderstanding of Jesus' words?

It is always possible to argue with the facts. In Jesus, however, there are facts that take us to task.

Reflection

Mark speaks clearly of who Jesus is and why he came, but he leaves it to his readers to decide on how to react. What does it mean to me that Jesus died and rose again?

JOHN TWISLETON

What do you want me to do for you?

Bartimaeus son of Timaeus, a blind beggar, was sitting by the roadside. When he heard that it was Jesus of Nazareth, he began to shout out and say, 'Jesus, Son of David, have mercy on me!'… Throwing off his cloak, he sprang up and came to Jesus. Then Jesus said to him, 'What do you want me to do for you?' The blind man said to him, 'My teacher, let me see again.' Jesus said to him, 'Go; your faith has made you well.' Immediately he regained his sight and followed him on the way.

As Mark arranged his sources using both his intellect and his faith, so our fully benefiting from his account of Jesus is more than just a matter of the intellect. We cannot look at the stories of Jesus purely objectively if Jesus is alive and beside us and touching our spirit.

Take blind Bartimaeus. His story has always had a moral for readers. 'Throwing off the cloak' has entered our language as an image of candour, letting others see where we are coming from. C.S. Lewis applauded honesty as the one essential prerequisite for prayer.

In asking Bartimaeus, 'What do you want me to do for you?' Jesus shows that he is not content to give unless we have the honesty to face our inadequacies and ask him to provide. Although a blind man had obvious need of physical healing, Bartimaeus is challenged about his intentions. Did he really want to be changed? Would he miss the revenue that his infirmity brought him as a beggar? Apparently not, for, in response to Jesus' questioning, the blind man said to him, 'My teacher, let me see again' (v. 51).

Bartimaeus received more than physical sight: he saw Jesus, the Son of God. His outer eye was opened but so was his inner eye, to the reason and purpose for life that Jesus brings.

Reflection

In Lourdes, on the zigzag path down to the Grotto, there is a statue of Bartimaeus that was placed there by an Italian who, although not cured of her blindness, rediscovered her faith, which, she realised, was more to be prized than physical sight.

JOHN TWISLETON

Venturesome faith

In the morning as they passed by, they saw the fig tree withered away to its roots. Then Peter remembered and said to him, 'Rabbi, look! The fig tree that you cursed has withered.' Jesus answered them, 'Have faith in God. Truly I tell you, if you say to this mountain, "Be taken up and thrown into the sea", and if you do not doubt in your heart, but believe that what you say will come to pass, it will be done for you. So I tell you, whatever you ask for in prayer, believe that you have received it, and it will be yours.'

If we are called to mountain-moving faith, it would seem, we should not complain about any molehills we stumble over!

That is one positive take on this challenging passage, which itself has points we could stumble over. What was Jesus doing cursing a fig tree, for example? This was no magical sign, but one of awesome significance. In cursing the tree, Jesus expressed God's judgement on the hard-heartedness of his fellow Israelites, who were often represented in the Old Testament by the image of a vine or tree.

Does Jesus not set faith against reason? Actually, 'have faith in faith' is not the point that Jesus is making. What he is saying is something like, 'If God shows you something that you need to pray for, hang on trustfully in prayer until it is granted to you.' The Son of God always remains the Son of Man. Jesus knows more than anyone what makes for human flourishing and is eager to provide it to his followers—even moving mountains if need be!

The verses here on faith and trust in God leap out with seeming eternal and universal relevance, although they sit in Mark's Gospel alongside the curious story of the fig tree. They raise a vital issue: how do we discern what it is we ought to pray for with 'mountain-moving faith'?

Reflection

Are there things weighing you down that you know deep down should be and could be lifted from you? Remember Jesus' words: 'Whatever you ask for in prayer, believe that you have received it, and it will be yours' (v. 24).

JOHN TWISLETON

Facing God's question

While Jesus was teaching in the temple, he said, 'How can the scribes say that the Messiah is the son of David? David himself, by the Holy Spirit, declared, "The Lord said to my Lord, 'Sit at my right hand, until I put your enemies under your feet.'" David himself calls him Lord; so how can he be his son?' And the large crowd was listening to him with delight.

One thing that comes across in Mark's Gospel more than in any of the other three accounts of Jesus' life is a certain shyness in Jesus concerning his divine origin. This fact is not in conflict with the representations given in the other Gospels, all of which appear to have had Mark's version as a base, and it has a ring of truth about it, given that Mark's is the earliest unadorned record of the historical Jesus. Reticent as he is about his Sonship, Jesus nevertheless gives a number of hints about it, among which our passage today is a prominent example.

In the other Gospels, this episode is set within a debate with Jewish leaders about the nature of the Messiah. Jesus' contemporaries expected the coming of a Saviour-Messiah of King David's dynasty, who would bring physical freedom to his people in bondage. Jesus presents verse 1 from Psalm 110, which indicates the Messiah is, in fact, above any human son. Since David himself calls him 'Lord', how can he be his son? The thrust of his teaching is that the Messiah will be more other-worldly than of this world.

In other words, the Son of Man is not just derived from humans but is also the Son of God and is referred to (as the Son of David is in this Psalm) as 'Lord God'. Jesus seemed to like a riddle. He enjoyed getting people questioning things from scripture. As we read this passage, we can hear once more his question to us: 'Who do you say that I am?' (Mark 8:29).

Reflection

As you reflect on the questions that people raised about God's Son, what questions would God's Son want you to address, so that you can better 'become participants in the divine nature' (2 Peter 1:4)?

JOHN TWISLETON

MARK 13:24–27 (NRSV)

The one who is to come

[Jesus said to his disciples] 'In those days, after that suffering, the sun will be darkened, and the moon will not give its light, and the stars will be falling from heaven, and the powers in the heavens will be shaken. Then they will see "the Son of Man coming in clouds" with great power and glory. Then he will send out the angels, and gather his elect from the four winds, from the ends of the earth to the ends of heaven.'

Christianity could never be invented by reason, although that is not to say it is unreasonable. It is something revealed—'the good news of Jesus Christ, the Son of God' (Mark 1:1). The whole edifice stands or falls on the person of Jesus, who himself reveals the love and purpose of God for the cosmos.

What does Jesus himself say about God's final purpose? These verses from the challenging chapter 13 speak of people being gathered for judgement. It is from Jesus' own lips that the Church completes her triple formula of faith: Christ has died, Christ is risen, Christ will come again.

When the Son of God appears on earth, Mark says, he adopts the familiar title 'Son of Man', which, as in today's passage, builds on the otherworldly Old Testament figure described in Daniel 7:13, weaving in the suffering servant theme that is a distinctive part of Jesus' teaching. His self-identification as both Son of God and Son of Man is primarily about the identity of a humble servant, but that does not prevent him from also fulfilling the traditional role of a divinely commissioned instrument of judgement.

The significance of Jesus is not just for a time; it is for eternity. So, our relationship with him, to say the least, determines our eternal happiness. That, it seems, is the personal challenge, invitation and blessing hidden behind the imagery of darkness, falling celestial bodies and shaking heavens.

Reflection

'I am convinced that neither death, nor life… nor powers, nor height, nor depth, nor anything else in all creation, will be able to separate us from the love of God in Christ Jesus our Lord' (Romans 8:38–39).

JOHN TWISLETON

This man was God's Son

At three o'clock Jesus cried out with a loud voice, 'Eloi, Eloi, lema sabachthani?' which means, 'My God, my God, why have you forsaken me?'... Then Jesus gave a loud cry and breathed his last... Now when the centurion, who stood facing him, saw that in this way he breathed his last, he said, 'Truly this man was God's Son!'

The cry of dereliction of the Son of Man has occupied theologians for 20 centuries. What can it mean for God to be forsaken by God? That cry led, within seconds, to a statement not from a theologian but from a professional killer, in the name of humanity, 'This man was God's Son!'

No doubt the centurion had seen hundreds die with curses from crucifixion, but Jesus breathed his last quoting scripture. 'My God, my God, why have you forsaken me?' is the first verse of Psalm 22, a prayer of both desolation and trust in God. Its repetition in Aramaic, Jesus' native tongue, rather than liturgical Hebrew, is evidence of how interior that prayer of abandonment had become.

Mark's Gospel begins by promising the good news of Jesus Christ, the Son of God (Mark 1:1). That good news is stated at this point of climax in the Gospel by a total outsider, whom we imagine catching the force of Jesus' humanity from his dying cry, humanity made the more forcefully convincing by his divinity.

Mark's Gospel is about who Jesus is, what he did for us and the impact this has on us. The story is full of encounters in which Jesus is unrecognised or partially recognised as the Son of God. His recognition by a total outsider is a fitting climax to a story that has drawn people into it for 20 centuries. As my own discussions with people who have read it show, it retains challenge and inspiration for readers in every age.

Prayer

Almighty God, who enlightened your holy Church through the inspired witness of your evangelist Mark, grant that we, being firmly grounded in the truth of the gospel, may be faithful to its teaching, both in word and deed; through Jesus Christ your Son our Lord, who is alive and reigns with you, in the unity of the Holy Spirit, one God, now and for ever.

Collect for the Feast of St Mark, *Common Worship*

JOHN TWISLETON

Word incarnate: John 1:1–18

The Prologue to John's Gospel is unlike any other part of the New Testament. In just a few verses, it contains the mystery of the incarnation—that is, how God became human. The same verses outline the fulfilment of all God's plans for his creation and provide the foundation for Christian hope. It is an extraordinary piece of writing, similar, perhaps, to a beautiful concerto with great movements of brilliance and insight that can only elicit our wonder and worship.

During these next few days, I hope to unfold some of these verses, considering what they mean in terms of Christian thinking about Jesus, especially with regard to his relationship with God, but I will also seek to ground them in life's experience.

It is not always easy to make the connections between big themes and our lives. They can seem too large to contain or remote and even irrelevant to everyday concerns. So, we will explore how what we believe about the God who contained the uncontainable in a baby has a great deal to say to us about hope, the value we put on material things and how we view God in relation to the toughest issues, such as suffering and dying. I also want to look at how John understood the newness of Christ's coming, particularly given the backdrop of fervour surrounding John the Baptist and the question of whether or not he was the Messiah. We will need to grasp something of how John understands the uniqueness of Jesus in relation to the Old Testament and especially Moses.

We will also explore some of the phrases that have—tragically—become almost toxic, in the way they have divided Christians. The phrase 'born again' has become a reference to the way we talk about our faith and the statements we make, rather than a description of the extraordinary miracle God performs as he draws us to himself and starts to change us completely.

Rather than simply building up a bank of knowledge as a kind of badge of honour, though, I hope these studies will act as a call to love and service. May God guide you into deeper thought, reflection and prayer.

Andy John

In the beginning

In the beginning was the Word, and the Word was with God, and the Word was God. He was in the beginning with God.

I can remember going to a visitor centre that had an interactive exhibition about the history of the Celtic people. There was a video presentation that lasted about ten minutes—a heady concoction of stories of tribal warfare and inter-clan rivalries. We were given a whistlestop tour of the last 2000 years of Celtic history and were told we had to peer back through the mists of time and understand who we were then in order to understand who we are now.

At the beginning of John's Gospel, too, we are invited to look back as far as we can in order to do much the same. We cannot understand what God is doing now without looking back to the 'beginning'.

John's Gospel is different from the other Gospels in many ways and its opening verses are unique. There is no account of the birth of Jesus or history of God's dealings with his people. Instead, we start at the start—a bit like Genesis—and what we find there is 'the Word'.

John is likely to have had several ideas about what he meant when he used this phrase, but the most obvious meaning is actually quite simple: that, from the very beginning, God has spoken and revealed himself, and this 'Word' has a real connection with God. He is the same as God, sharing eternity, sharing identity and sharing purpose.

This means that the whole book must be read and understood in that light. The Galilean would be no magician, no soothsayer. He would not be another prophet in a long line of holy people. He is nothing less than God, speaking God's words, doing God's works, and he has plans for the world, for you and for me.

Prayer

Gracious God, your Word is from all eternity. You have revealed yourself to all people and shown yourself as Lord Almighty. Speak again, so I may hear afresh what things both great and small you wish me to hear. Amen

ANDY JOHN

The light of all people

All things came into being through him, and without him not one thing came into being. What has come into being in him was life and the life was the light of all people.

Some of us may recall the undignified role we were sometimes given at school of being a 'gopher'. There were no mobiles or online messenger service in those days! Our task was to carry a note from one class and teacher to another, and that was the extent of our responsibility. There was nothing great or creative about it; we were the passive bearers of another's words.

In the few words that make up today's passage, however, John seeks to draw out the meaning of the idea he has given us in his opening sentences. He does this by using the idea of an agent—that is, someone who acts on another's behalf. He is not merely the bearer of news or a message as we were, though, but the active agent, bringing into being the things God wishes.

The meaning is clear: God's full and unimpeded Lordship over all creation is revealed through his Word. 'Not one thing' are the words John uses to emphasise the full extent of his sovereign reign. If God is seen to be sovereign by the work of his Word, then he can have no equals. If the reign of God is fully revealed by his actions, then he has no peers and no competitors.

It is only implicit at this stage, but we can see two themes emerging: the greatness of Jesus and the possibility of a relationship with God through him. We will find John drawing out both themes as we work through this chapter, but, for now, let us hold the weight of these extraordinary truths in our mind's eye. This is the true greatness of God, who is worthy of endless praise and adoration.

Prayer

Lord of all creation, you sustain in being all that is and none can compare with you. As you spoke and brought life into existence, speak into the smallness of our own lives so that something of your greatness may be known and worshipped, through Jesus Christ our Lord. Amen

ANDY JOHN

Not understood, not overcome

> The light shines in the darkness and the darkness did not comprehend it (NASB) [or '… did not overcome it', NRSV].

John has told us that the source of all life is God's Word, by whose power everything has come into being, and this life is the very essence of what makes people unique: 'The life was the light of all people', he says (v. 4). Now he draws this line of thought to a close by using a clever word that can mean two things—and he probably intends us to understand it as having both meanings.

The first meaning is that of 'understood'. The darkness (by which John means all that is not God) has not 'understood' the light because light and darkness are opposites and mutually excluding. The darkness cannot perceive or make sense of something so utterly alien to it that they remain apart.

The second meaning is that of 'overcome' (or, as the Good News Bible has it, 'the darkness has never put it out'). The meaning here is that of power or enduring force. The darkness cannot overwhelm the light because the light will always pierce the gloom. To put it another way, darkness cannot remain dark when it is touched by the rays of light.

In both of these meanings, John intends us to see the enduring strength and might of Christ. The reality of God's apparent absence might seem overwhelming, but light still invades the darkness and transforms it.

Across the years, I have encountered people who find this truth to be personally important. Patients in hospital, those facing awful crises or uncertainty, damaged lives that appear to be impervious to hope suddenly discover the light piercing their own darkness. This is not in any way to diminish their challenges, but, rather, to set out the hope we have in God. The gospel of Christ means that lives and hopeless situations can be transformed.

Prayer

Come, gentle Saviour and Light of the World. Shine light into hidden places long absent from your love and let that light settle, heal and restore your own good image in us. Amen

ANDY JOHN

His name was John

There was a man sent from God, whose name was John. He came as a witness to testify to the light, so that all might believe through him.

Having set his Gospel in the widest context—that of all eternity—John now focuses down on to recent history and the ministry of John the Baptist. The early Christian communities would have known all the stories about John—his message of repentance, baptism and his affirming of Jesus as the Messiah. It is not surprising, therefore, that John's ministry provides a marker for placing the story of Jesus in recent history.

The Baptist's ministry is to draw attention to Jesus, to 'testify to the light'. In other words, he shines the spotlight away from himself and towards another. The reason for doing so is that people might believe in Jesus. The testimony of another person strengthens the claims that anyone might make about themselves.

Drawing our attention to John serves a double purpose, of course. First, it reminds us of people's expectations: the Messiah, long promised, was near and the Baptist now announces his coming. It also highlights John as an example to us. John did not advance himself and his ministry, but pointed to Jesus. This is a model for all Christians, although it is a good deal easier to say this than to do it!

In traditional Christian thought, the sin of pride led to Lucifer's fall, and few honest leaders would deny that pride is the most dangerous and beguiling of sins. John shows us that lowliness is a worthy response to Christ. How often, I wonder, do we claim credit for something that is not ours but God's? Even if we do have a share in advancing the gospel, are we content simply to rejoice in the privilege that is ours?

This is the question John's ministry asks of us.

Prayer

Gracious God, as you gave John the task of pointing others to Jesus, let my life reflect his worth and goodness. In speech and words, in manners and attitudes, make me like Jesus. I ask it in his name. Amen

ANDY JOHN

A witness

He himself was not the light, but he came to testify to the light. The true light, which enlightens everyone, was coming into the world.

In yesterday's passage we saw how John the Baptist pointed to Jesus, the true Messiah, and away from himself, lest anyone think that John himself was the promised Saviour. It appears that this might have been a problem in some communities because the Gospel writer makes this point very clearly. John the Baptist 'was not the light' (v. 8); he was not the Messiah but, rather, the messenger. It would have been a double source of grief and confusion if any had believed that John was the Messiah and that he had died without any sign of God's vindication. That God would not vindicate his chosen one was unthinkable. The Gospel writer ensures that any lingering doubts about the Baptist's ministry and status are dispelled.

This gospel truth is given new meaning in today's passage: 'The true light, which enlightens everyone, was coming into the world' (v. 9). We often use words such as 'atonement' and 'sacrifice' in relation to the saving work of Jesus on the cross, and these concepts are vital, but the passage above presents things slightly differently, showing how God gives true understanding. The word used for 'enlighten' was one that came from the Greek world, where understanding and knowledge were believed to be especially important. To 'know' was to be powerful and, thus, liberated to exercise influence. We can see how this might help John explain the truth about Jesus because, without 'knowing' who Jesus is and his true nature, we know him either partially or not at all.

Of course, this is not a stand-alone idea for the bright and clever. Any suggestion that simply amassing knowledge about Jesus is sufficient turns the rest of the New Testament on its head. Knowledge can be open to abuse and the idolatrous exercise of power. Its importance lies in the way God gives true understanding, which means knowing who Jesus really is.

Prayer

Lord God, you open eyes and ears so that your Son is known and worshipped. May my inner being, opened by your Spirit, perceive the one who is Lord of all, in and through the whole of creation. Amen

ANDY JOHN

Made through him

> He was in the world, and the world came into being through him;
> yet the world did not know him. He came to what was his own and
> his own people did not accept him.

In the bidding prayers used at a traditional service of lessons and carols
in Advent or during the Christmas season, we pray for 'all those who
know not the Lord Jesus, or who love him not, or who by sin have
grieved his heart of love'. I find these words deeply moving because they
convey some of the heartache in God for his creation.

In today's passage, we hear similar words and they too convey a kind
of pain. The Gospel writer continues by moving from the person called
to proclaim God to the nation called to do the same. Here, the fourth
Gospel sits closely with the others in terms of the way in which Jesus is
announced as Israel's Saviour, and the force of these words comes from
the way in which Jesus is rejected. The book of Isaiah contains the
famous words, familiar perhaps from Handel's great work, *Messiah*, that
God's servant was 'despised and rejected by men; a man of sorrows,
and acquainted with grief; and as one from whom men hide their faces
he was despised, and we esteemed him not' (Isaiah 53:3, ESV).

There are many reasons Jesus is rejected today. Some people believe
that faith is ridiculous, others do not see how Jesus is relevant to them
and still others consider his call so all-embracing that it is too much to
bear. While it is not really any kind of comfort, knowing that the rejection of Jesus has a wider context and history and being aware of this
bigger picture may help us when he is still rejected today. Although it
will not always be so (Philippians 2:10–11), somehow in the mystery of
God the rejection of Jesus, witnessed in his life and death, continues
and the world still does 'not know him' (v. 10).

Prayer

*Lord Jesus, rejected by people, but glorious in heaven, let me be captivated
afresh by your grace and, so inspired, give a good account of my trust in
you. For your praise and glory. Amen*

ANDY JOHN

Children of God

But to all who received him, who believed in his name, he gave power to become children of God, who were born, not of blood or of the will of the flesh or of the will of man, but of God.

In today's passage John lays out the glorious truth of our salvation, which is God's doing and not our own. At first sight it might seem strange to list obvious but irrelevant sources for such a thing—born 'not of blood or of the will of flesh' (v. 13)—but John has an important point in mind. It is that grace is transmitted by neither race nor inheritance, nor by any other human means, but is the free gift of God (Ephesians 2:8).

The image of being reborn or born again will be used powerfully a little later in this Gospel (chapter 3). It describes an act so instrumental in defining who we are and so transforming in its effects that nothing less than a picture of new life and birth will suffice. Christians have not always agreed on how this happens and it is sad that such an extraordinary image has become a divisive issue. Given the significance of the phrase, it cannot be true that there are 'born again' Christians and 'not born again' Christians. To belong to Christ, we must all be born again. If we are his, we are born again, irrespective of what others may say.

It is all made a little easier if we focus not on the 'when' or 'how' we came to Christ and received new birth, but, rather, on the fact that we have indeed received Christ and been born again. Christians who receive this free gift of grace and understand it as such are less likely to judge others. When we remember that the important matter for Christ is how such faith is living in us and producing the fruit of his grace, it restores this wonderful image to its rightful place.

Prayer

Lord Jesus, we offer praise and honour to you, for we are yours by grace and your gift of new birth. May the fruit of your grace overflow in me for your greater glory. Amen

ANDY JOHN

We have seen his glory

And the Word became flesh and lived among us, and we have seen his glory, the glory as of a father's only son, full of grace and truth.

Family photos can reveal a great deal. We see likenesses of children in their parents that are hard to quantify. Something of mum or dad lives in their offspring in the most uncanny way. This is a picture we might hold on to as we explore the extraordinary words in today's passage.

There are few Bible verses that have more weight than John 1:14. We are told how God's Word, the agent of his creation and means of relating to the world, became human. Yet, somehow, he retained his divine nature, reflecting God's own image and essence, full of grace and truth.

John brings several strands together in this verse. First, God stepped into human history when he 'became flesh and lived among us'. Second, the uniqueness of Jesus, the 'only son', is announced. Third, the 'incarnate God' (that is, God become human) remains fully God—bearing his likeness, reflecting his glory.

We can say that in this is the very essence of the gospel. Christians believe that Jesus' life and ministry, his teaching and miracles and his death and resurrection all make sense because he was no 'mere man'. Jesus understands our every weakness (Hebrews 4:15), but, because he is God in nature, he is able to do a great deal about our weaknesses, our sins and our mortality. If this is true for individuals, it is true for all people and all history, too, because God is 'in the world' and not apart from it.

It is this that makes faith in Christ so compelling. God truly has come to us and, from within our humanity, redeems and saves us. The old saying retains its power still: the Son of God became the Son of Man so that the sons and daughters of man might become sons and daughters of God.

Prayer

Lord Jesus Christ, you know our every weakness and we rejoice in your saving strength to win us. Praise to you, Father, Son and Holy Spirit, one gracious and holy God, world without end. Amen

Andy John

JOHN 1:15 (NRSV)

Three in one

John testified to him and cried out, 'This was he of whom I said, "He who comes after me ranks ahead of me because he was before me."'

We have already seen how John attaches the coming of Jesus to the ministry of John the Baptist, which allows him to place Jesus in a story that would have been familiar to many. We see, too, that God has been at work in a continuous way—the birth of Jesus marking the start of something altogether new and wonderful.

It would be easy to see these words as simply a kind of repetition of what was recorded earlier, namely that John's whole ministry was to announce the coming of the Messiah. They would therefore only reinforce something previously stated, but there is a real point to them. The words 'because he was before me' must mean more than simply Jesus ranks higher than John. What we have here is a further statement about the pre-existence of Jesus. If John 1:1 introduced the idea, placing the statement on the lips of John the Baptist gives it stronger force because it becomes part of a narrative so familiar to the early Christians—and makes it more central, too.

Some people struggle with the idea that Jesus was divine and with what became known as the doctrine of the Trinity. Mental gymnastics threaten to overwhelm the metaphors and pointers we see in scripture, but these remain undeniable. I have already referred to the bidding prayer for the traditional service of lessons and carols. The final reading from John 1 in that service is entitled 'St John unfolds the mystery of the Incarnation', which beautifully balances how the mystery remains and yet declares it to be true. This should lead us to see two things: that God is truly three in one and his sovereign rule allows him to operate and reveal his nature on his own terms. Second, just as the angels saw and proclaimed, God is worthy of all praise and glory in the highest places.

Prayer

Blessed Father, you gave your Son so the world might be redeemed and believe. He is your very image and worthy with you and the Holy Spirit of eternal praise and glory. Amen

ANDY JOHN

Grace on grace

From his fullness we have all received, grace upon grace.

From where I lived as a child, it was possible to see much of the expanse of Cardigan Bay—a huge area encompassing most of the Irish Sea. On a good day, I could see the most southerly parts of Wales and also the Lleyn Peninsula to the north, taking in Snowdon for good measure. It never ceased to leave me awestruck, so vast and great was the territory. I suspect people who work in fields such as astronomy or marine biology feel a bit like this as they contemplate the vastness of their subject matter.

In today's reading, I think John intends us to be struck by the scale of God's grace. The superlatives he uses press home the sheer wonder of God's goodness to his creation. First, from his 'fullness' we have 'all' received. In God's economy there are no half measures, only fullness. What God gives to his creation is nothing less than his very self and in his entirety. It is also to *all* his creation he gives, so that, potentially, no one is excluded from knowing Jesus' love. A little later in this Gospel (in chapter 3) we will read how God loved the world so much that he gave his only Son for its salvation. The generosity of that truth is anticipated here.

Second, this vast and generous gift is endless; it is a 'grace upon grace'. I have often wondered what these words mean and I am still a little unsure. Undoubtedly, God's blessings are always new and keep coming so that we may explore them for all time. I wonder if these words also anticipate the coming of the Holy Spirit, because the Spirit is the one whose work among us continues each day. If this is correct, we have, again, early seeds of the Trinity here: God the Father sending the Son, Christ, to live among us, and the Spirit anticipated as the means by which lives are renewed in grace.

Prayer

Gracious God, may we all today receive the grace you have promised from the fullness that is yours and may we rejoice in the wonder of your goodness. Amen

ANDY JOHN

Grace and truth

> The law indeed was given through Moses; grace and truth came through Jesus Christ.

Today is the first occasion in John's Gospel when the writer refers back to what will become a recurring theme, namely that the old revelation and way of obeying God have been superseded. This backward glance allows John to make a contrast and reinforce his message about the wonder of grace that has been revealed in Jesus.

Here we must remember that John is not telling us that the law was a bad thing. It is easy to read the Bible as though the coming of Christ was a sort of Plan B because Plan A (the law) had failed so miserably. A more helpful way of thinking about this would be to see how the law operated and pointed to grace as God's enduring approach to his creation. The law never cancelled the gracious promises to Abraham (Genesis 15:1–6), which, from the beginning, were about faith in God's goodness. So, how was that covenant of grace maintained? It was through the law! The regulations allowed choices to be made that reflected God's good standards and showed where people fell short, but also how they could continue in faith.

John's contrast, then, is not between what is good and what is bad, but is a way of demonstrating that grace has come to us in Jesus, just as the law came through Moses. In other words, Jesus is the greater mediator of the blessings of God. Once more there is an implied pointing to the work of the Spirit because obedience would no longer be a matter of following a written code as our first guide, but following the Spirit and the new law of liberty.

Today we could respond to this by asking how grace shows itself in our lives. If we have received grace from Jesus, is that evident in our lives and in what way?

Prayer

Lord Jesus Christ, giver of grace, let your life and goodness control and direct my life so that, in and through me, your reign may be seen and extended. I ask this for your sake. Amen

ANDY JOHN

God has made himself known

No one has ever seen God. It is God the only Son, who is close to the Father's heart, who has made him known.

On this Christmas Day, I wish you a merry Christmas and that Jesus will fill you with the joy of his birth and the wonder of his coming. Today's verse is a fitting place to conclude this series of passages and the NRSV's translation here is especially powerful.

I would like to draw out two important points, the first concerning the disclosure of God. We know in the Old Testament that Moses looked on God's glory but only saw his back (Exodus 33:23). John is conscious of this and draws a contrast between Jesus and Moses again. Whereas Moses saw God only partially, Jesus has seen him and known him perfectly. This allows him, secondly, to set out the uniqueness of Jesus, not only in his own nature but because of his relationship to the Father: it is God the Son, the only Son, who has made God known.

In our world, where so much is dispensable or an 'optional extra', we see that, in the great plan of God's salvation, Jesus stands centre stage; there is no one else like him, nor could there ever be.

Knowing that this is the big picture has consequences for our lives. We can have true confidence in the faith that is Christ's gift to us. No one compares to Jesus and the way in which he makes God known to us. More than that, we have the hope we need to press on in faith, because, in Jesus, God is known more completely, thus increasing our love for him and renewing our service in glad and grateful obedience.

The Christmas message announces that a child contained the uncontainable so that human lives might be transformed into God's very likeness. This is what it means to know and love God. This is why the gospel is good and Christmas is a joyful celebration.

Prayer

You are the Saviour of the world, Lord Jesus Christ, born to save us from our sins, showing us the Father's glory. All praise to you on this and every day. Amen

ANDY JOHN

Praying with Psalm 1

Thimbles, teaspoons, beer mats, stamps... it is amazing what people collect. Items of no obvious cash value can be of immense importance to enthusiasts. While those who do not share their passion may fail to see the point or even ridicule the avid collector, we can see that, sometimes, a committed few have been responsible for preserving invaluable and inspirational collections for future generations.

We should, for example, be immeasurably grateful that among our ancient forebears in faith there were some who collected Hebrew poetry, gathering the poems together into books. Some were poems of lament, others were outpourings of thanksgiving; many were hymns, composed to be sung in communal gatherings of worship, remembrance and celebration. We should be grateful, too, that, more than five centuries before the birth of Jesus Christ, someone had the vision to collect these collections. In doing so, they compiled what became one of the most cherished books of the Bible, the Psalms.

Despite their ancient origins and the fact that some of their Hebrew poetic style is inevitably lost in translation, these poems speak to us. They speak of YHWH, our almighty creator and sustainer. They also give us a language with which to speak with him. So, while the Psalms contain words from God and about God, they also include words to God. They give us a vocabulary of praise, grief, doubt, trust, anger, thanksgiving and much more. What an awe-inspiring privilege that the Psalms are available to us.

Jesus himself was intimately acquainted with the Psalms. Paul encouraged the early believers to use them to encourage, teach and caution one another (Colossians 3:16). Where better, then, to turn for inspiration and guidance for our prayer life than the Psalms and what better place to start than the simple and succinct verses we know as Psalm 1?

Believers of every generation have meditated on the unpretentious wisdom of Psalm 1. This week, using various translations and some readings from elsewhere in the Psalms and beyond, we shall follow in their footsteps. As we do so, may the words of one of Jesus' first disciples be our earnest prayer: 'Lord, teach us to pray' (Luke 11:1).

Steve Aisthorpe

Prayer of thanksgiving

> Oh, the joys of those who do not follow the advice of the wicked, or stand around with sinners, or join in with mockers. But they delight in the law of the Lord, meditating on it day and night. They are like trees planted along the riverbank, bearing fruit each season. Their leaves never wither, and they prosper in all they do.

I wonder when you last experienced a moment of wonder. Perhaps over these last days, as people around the globe have celebrated the single most wonder-filled event in history, the time when 'the Word became flesh and made his dwelling among us' (John 1:14, NIV), you have experienced hints of wonder, that feeling of awe and astonishment. Perhaps, like the writer of Psalm 8, you have gazed into the unfathomable depths of a night sky and been moved to reverence and thanksgiving: 'When I consider your heavens, the work of your fingers, the moon and the stars, which you have set in place… Lord, our Lord, how majestic is your name in all the earth!' (Psalm 8:3, 9, NIV). It is with this kind of profound wonder and gratitude that Psalm 1 begins.

Most translations struggle to express the emphatic and overwhelmingly positive sense of awe in the opening phrase. Some begin with 'Happy are those' (GNB), others with 'Blessed is the one' (NIV). Perhaps something like, 'Wow, the blessedness of those' would better capture the essence of what is being expressed.

This happiness is not the superficial satisfaction of pleasant feelings, but, rather, the deep joy of a life lived well in the ways of the Creator. It is the kind of life offered by, and in relationship with, Jesus Christ: 'My purpose is to give them a rich and satisfying life' (John 10:10, NLT).

As we read this psalm, we are challenged to walk in the ways of the Lord and consistently choose the path that we believe will most please him. We should also be amazed and humbled by the offer of a satisfying life of delight and filled with appreciation.

Reflection

If the only prayer you ever say in your whole life is 'thank you', that would suffice.

Meister Eckhart
STEVE AISTHORPE

Prayer for discernment

> Happy are those who reject the advice of evil people, who do not follow the example of sinners or join those who have no use for God. Instead, they find joy in obeying the law of the Lord, and they study it day and night. They are like trees that grow beside a stream, that bear fruit at the right time, and whose leaves do not dry up. They succeed in everything they do. But evil people are not like this at all; they are like straw that the wind blows away.

A GP friend vented his frustration to me at having to spend so much time dealing with the outcomes of people's poor choices. While there are diseases and accidents that can overtake anyone at any time, health services in Western countries are often burdened by the consequences of foolish, reckless or just unwise decisions. Our choices influence our physical and mental health. Psalm 1 reminds us that our very souls are also shaped by the choices we make.

Psalm 1 is adamant that the consequence for those who consistently refuse to be aligned with cynics and reject the influences of 'those who have no use for God' (v. 1) is an indescribably wonderful contentment and wholeness.

The earliest 'instruction book' for Christians, The Didache, written around AD60–140, begins with the reminder that 'there are two ways, one of life and one of death, and there is a great difference between these two ways.' Our lives comprise and are shaped by a multitude of choices. Choices become habits—and habits grow into lifestyles. Psalm 1 exhorts us to embrace a two-stranded approach that will lead to life as God intends it, avoiding destructive influences and investing time in the transforming influence of the scriptures.

With the end of another year on the horizon, it is an appropriate time to review the influences on our lives, to take a look at the advice we follow, the examples we emulate and the company we keep.

Prayer

Father, please give me wisdom to discern what is good and helpful and what is negative and destructive; grant me the courage and discipline to reject the unhelpful and cultivate the good. Amen

STEVE AISTHORPE

ROMANS 12:1–2 (JB PHILLIPS, ABRIDGED)

Praying to go deeper

With eyes wide open to the mercies of God, I beg you... as an act of intelligent worship, to give him your bodies, as a living sacrifice, consecrated to him and acceptable by him. Don't let the world around you squeeze you into its own mould, but let God re-mould your minds from within, so that you may prove in practice that the plan of God for you is good, meets all his demands and moves towards the goal of true maturity.

It may seem strange in a week focused on Psalm 1 to take today's passage from Paul's letter to the Romans. However, what the psalmist exhorts us to do because of the inspiring vision of the awesome blessing that is on offer, Paul also urges us to do in grateful response to God's incredible mercy, which has been poured out for us through the life, death and resurrection of Jesus.

What the psalmist has counselled in encouraging us to avoid the influence of the 'wicked', 'sinners' and 'mockers' (Psalm 1:1, NLT), Paul summarises in his phrase, 'Don't let the world around you squeeze you into its own mould.' Paul longs for his readers to be changed by a transformation of the mind, and the writer of Psalm 1 gives practical directions regarding how this can occur. Having rejected particular sources of advice, certain examples and the company of those opposed to God and his ways, we are, instead, to delight in the scriptures. We are urged to cultivate a habit of consistent contemplation of scripture: 'delight in the law of the Lord, meditating on it day and night' (v. 2).

Studying the scriptures with the aim of understanding them intellectually is valuable and important, but meditation is different. Just as we might slowly savour a delicious meal, allowing our taste buds to appreciate each mouthful, so in meditation we allow the words of scripture to sink slowly into our souls. This may involve quietly repeating the words or using our imagination to place ourselves in a particular Bible story, asking God to lead us into a deeper understanding of truth.

Prayer
Lord, please give me a new joy in your word and lead me into a deeper encounter with you. Amen

STEVE AISTHORPE

Roots and fruits

Blessed is the man who walks not in the counsel of the ungodly, nor stands in the path of sinners, nor sits in the seat of the scornful; but his delight is in the law of the Lord and in his law he meditates day and night. He shall be like a tree planted by the rivers of water that brings forth its fruit in its season, whose leaf also shall not wither; and whatever he does shall prosper. The ungodly are not so, but are like the chaff which the wind drives away.

When someone says that things are 'like chalk and cheese', nobody doubts the meaning: they are radically different, poles apart. Even so, while from a distance chalk and cheese might easily be confused, it would be inconceivable to miss the total contrast between the two images given here, of a healthy, fruitful tree (v. 3) and dry, wind-blown chaff (v. 4).

The tree, presented as a simile for a person who rejects evil and embraces God's ways, is not just any tree. It is not the consequence of seed blown at random; it has been planted with care beside life-giving water. While it experiences the usual seasons, with their inherent challenges and blessings, it is fruitful. Its roots draw on an abundant supply of living water, providing stability in the face of inevitable storms. What a vivid contrast between this and the lifeless, transient chaff, which is a simile for those who reject God.

Taken in isolation, the phrase 'whatever they do prospers' could suggest a simple guarantee to the faithful. Wider reading in the Psalms and beyond dispels such an illusion, and underlines the value of sinking our roots deep into the source of all wisdom. The alluring image of the tree reminds us of Jesus' invitation: 'Let anyone who is thirsty come to me and drink' (John 7:37, NIV). He is the source of 'living water' (4:10) and we are invited, through prayer, to tap into divine resources that yield the fruit of Christ-like character (Galatians 5:22–23).

Reflection

'Just as you received Christ Jesus as Lord, continue to live your lives in him, rooted and built up in him, strengthened in the faith as you were taught' (Colossians 2:6–7).

Steve Aisthorpe

PSALM 1:1–6 (NIV)

The prayer of tears

Blessed is the one who does not walk in step with the wicked or stand in the way that sinners take or sit in the company of mockers, but whose delight is in the law of the Lord, and who meditates on his law day and night. That person is like a tree planted by streams of water, which yields its fruit in season and whose leaf does not wither—whatever they do prospers. Not so the wicked! They are like chaff that the wind blows away. Therefore the wicked will not stand in the judgment, nor sinners in the assembly of the righteous. For the Lord watches over the way of the righteous, but the way of the wicked leads to destruction.

If we are honest, this first Psalm has parts that we like, parts that inspire and encourage us, but it also has verses we struggle with. Like many of the Psalms, there are verses that are uncomfortable to our 21st-century ears; they offend our modern sensibilities. Perhaps we can come to terms with divine judgment and its consequences as abstract notions, but if we allow ourselves to dwell on them and permit our minds to ponder their implications, we cannot help but be moved. Surely we will experience a profound sadness as we reflect on the fact that there are, indeed, people who choose a path of blatant rebellion against God and his ways.

While we can draw substantial encouragement from the facts that 'his works are perfect, and all his ways are just' (Deuteronomy 32:4) and that 'the Lord is compassionate and gracious, slow to anger and abounding in love' (Psalm 103:8), no serious reading of the Bible can leave us in doubt that we should be acutely concerned for the well-being and destiny of people who appear to be determined to live in opposition to God. Jesus himself, faced with those who seemed oblivious to the ways God had revealed, was moved to tears (Luke 19:41).

Reflection

'In the same way, the Spirit helps us in our weakness. We do not know what we ought to pray for, but the Spirit himself intercedes for us through wordless groans' (Romans 8:26).

STEVE AISTHORPE

The Prayer of Examen

You have searched me, Lord, and you know me. You know when I sit and when I rise; you perceive my thoughts from afar. You discern my going out and my lying down; you are familiar with all my ways. Before a word is on my tongue you, Lord, know it completely. You hem me in behind and before, and you lay your hand upon me. Such knowledge is too wonderful for me, too lofty for me to attain. Where can I go from your Spirit? Where can I flee from your presence?... Search me, God, and know my heart.

All who venture across the ocean know the importance of meticulous navigation. Setting off in the right direction is important, but maintaining the right course by means of a conscientious routine of checks is also crucial. Today's reading reminds us that God closely observes our hearts —and Psalm 1 challenges us regarding the direction of our life. Are we going with the flow or ensuring that regular contemplation of scripture informs our decisions? Are we in danger of being blown off course?

While Psalm 1 prompts us to set off in the right direction, it also reminds us of the importance of regular examinations. Ignatius Loyola (1491–1556), founder of the Society of Jesus (Jesuits), suggested that a key to developing a healthy spiritual life is the regular habit of pausing to reflect prayerfully on the day. What he called the Prayer of Examen can be applied just as well to the year that is drawing to a close.

The Examen has four components. First, we focus on the presence of God: 'The Lord is near to all who call on him' (Psalm 145:18). Then, we prayerfully review the day (or year) that has passed, giving thanks for good things. Third, we try to discern how God has been at work, when we were most conscious of his presence, when we think we pleased him or disappointed him. Finally, we respond. This response might be in the form of practical action, thanksgiving, repentance, a resolution or anything that flows genuinely from our prayerful review.

Prayer

'Search me, God, and know my heart; test me and know my anxious thoughts. See if there is any offensive way in me, and lead me in the way everlasting' (Psalm 139:23–24).

STEVE AISTHORPE

Supporting
Who Let The Dads Out?
with a gift in your will

For many charities, income from legacies is crucial in enabling them to plan ahead, and often provides the funding to develop new projects. A legacy to support BRF's ministry would make a huge difference.

Who Let The Dads Out? (www.wholetthedadsout.org.uk) has the potential to make a significant impact on the lives of families, churches and whole communities. It is a catalyst enabling effective missional outreach and ministry to fathers and father figures and their children. Its vision is simple: 'Turning the hearts of fathers to their children and the hearts of children to their fathers' (Malachi 4:6).

Starting with fathers and toddlers, Who Let The Dads Out? groups can develop a range of ministry opportunities with these men, with the result that:

- **Families are strengthened** as dads engage in parenting their children and therefore engage better with their partners in the role of parents.
- **Communities are invigorated** as men develop a stronger network of friends within the local community, helping in the process of binding a community together.
- **Christian faith is passed from one generation to the next** as the church engages with fathers, encourages them to explore faith issues and challenges them to teach their own values and beliefs to their children.

Throughout its history, BRF's ministry has been enabled thanks to the generosity of those who have shared its vision and supported its work, both by giving during their lifetime and also through legacy gifts.

A legacy gift would help fund the development and sustainability of BRF's Who Let The Dads Out? ministry into the future. We hope you may consider a legacy gift to help us continue to take this work forward.

For further information about making a gift to BRF in your will or to discuss how a specific bequest could be used to develop our ministry, please contact Sophie Aldred (Head of Fundraising) or Richard Fisher (Chief Executive) by email at fundraising@brf.org.uk or by phone on 01865 319700.

This page is intentionally left blank.

The BRF
Magazine

Messy Church in 2014

Lucy Moore

Ten years ago, in April 2004, the very first Messy Church was held at St Wilfrid's, Cowplain, near Portsmouth. We asked its founder, Lucy Moore, for her thoughts on the past ten years and the possible future for Messy Church.

What were your expectations for Messy Church back in 2004?

When we held our first Messy Church, we had absolutely no idea it would be the start of such a wild adventure and that over 2000 churches would join us in our messiness. We only started it for our own parish families and are still bemused that it's headed off in so many different directions. The original Messy Church is still going strong: I was down on my knees poking birdseed out of the skirting board crevices only last week, after a riotous session with new families exploring baptism and old familiar friends who have been with us all the way through. One eleven-year-old, Phoebe, after belonging to this congregation since she was a baby, has just decided to come on to the leadership team.

Why do you think Messy Church has grown like this?

I think it can only be God's Spirit wanting it to happen, longing for the church to understand what church is really for. I know that he's worked through the Fresh Expressions movement, with whom we are now happily Associate Partners. Fresh Expressions encouraged churches to risk being church differently, and spread the story of Messy Church across the world before we were in a position to do so ourselves. Also, it's grown through gossip—one Christian gossiping a good thing to another or one family gossiping the good time they've had at their Messy Church to another family and bringing them along to the next session.

I think, too, that an honest engagement with the needs of families outside the church has meant that the church has tried to meet those needs rather than being hampered by trying to get people to 'do church as we do it', and this has also resulted in growth. And of course, BRF's excellent resourcing in the background has meant great back-up for publicity, design, books and all things legal where I would be out of my depth, like trademarking and copyrighting.

What is BRF's role in this?

My theory is that God put this idea into BRF because it was the perfect organisation to help it grow, like the 'good ground' in the parable of the sower. BRF provides the aforementioned resources and office back-up that enable Jane, Martyn and me to get on with the face-to-face ministry. BRF gives us the space to talk about the ministry at a deeper level and understands how important people are to making things work well. It isn't 'owned' by any particular denomination but is respected by a wide spectrum of denominations, so we can happily work alongside most Christian churches. It also has a faithful foundation of praying friends: in the Messy Church growth, we're reaping the hours, days, weeks and years you've spent committing BRF and its ministry to God.

What do the next ten years look like?

Of course we have no idea! If you'd asked us this question ten years ago, we wouldn't have dared dream of anything like the reality. I'll be even wrinklier in another ten, so I hope we'll have found funding to bring some young, lively, wise people on to the BRF team to keep us in touch with the ongoing needs of families and young people. There will probably be continued numerical growth—maybe up to 4000 Messy Churches by 2024—but this must flatten out eventually. I think we'll have a whole range of tried-and-tested resources for helping families move on in faith. I hope we'll have found great ways of helping older children and teenagers stay on board as leaders. Probably the established church will be taking us seriously if we've survived that long, so there should be many more paid professionals working full-time in Messy Churches. I'd like to think we'd have full-time coordinators in several countries across the world, too. In ten years, there could be two generations of families who have grown up thinking that Messy Church is the norm rather than the exception to the rule, so it will have evolved naturally to meet their (for now) unimaginable needs and to make the most of the (for now) unimaginable technology.

How can BRF supporters be part of this development?

Please continue to pray, to keep that good ground well fertilised. Help us to find ways of putting the ministry on a more secure financial footing: to survive the next decade, we must be less reliant on the very few *very* generous people who currently fund us: we need a broader base of individuals and churches giving a little regularly. Do keep being proud of us: we love being part of the BRF family and are always very touched when any of you take the trouble to tell friends about our work or to encourage us personally with a letter or email. Thank you for all you do.

Ten reasons to go on retreat

Daniel Muñoz

In his 2012 book *Falling Upward*, the American Franciscan Richard Rohr explores spirituality from the perspective of 'the two halves of life'. The first half is what he describes as the time of learning, focusing on the outer world and developing our own personal identity. The second half is the time of unlearning, focusing on the inner world and reconnecting with God in deeper, more transformational ways. In fact, he says, this latter dimension of the second half of life stands at the heart of religion (in Latin, *re-ligio*, meaning 'reconnect').

In my experience as a priest, first in parish ministry and now as chaplain of Los Olivos retreat centre in Spain, whether we find ourselves in the first or the second half of life, our deepest human need is to reconnect with ourselves, with God and with the world around us in ways that are life-giving. I have seen this, especially, in the many people who have come to Los Olivos over the last few years. So, although the reasons why people come on retreat are very varied, most share a similar experience of reconnecting with God, oneself and others in new ways.

Now, a personal confession. I am not a great believer in anything that sells itself as 'ten (or any other number) easy steps' to lose weight, find love, be successful in life, or whatever. In fact, whenever I read articles advocating easy recipes or steps to change my life, my first reaction is one of scepticism and suspicion. Because this article gives you ten reasons for going on retreat, a word of warning is required. These are not the top ten reasons why retreats are great and can change your life. Nor is it an exhaustive list to sum up all that a retreat can offer. Instead, these are just some of the most recurring themes, motivations and benefits that those who have come on retreat to Los Olivos have shared with us. I pray you will find them helpful.

- Connecting with your inner self: Retreats offer you a safe space to look inside and do some necessary inner work. This can be done through times of silence, personal reflection, guided meditation and prayerful exercises. A good retreat will enable you to reconnect with your inner self and to create space for God to reconnect with you.

- Recharging your batteries: Retreat times are not just beneficial for our spiritual life. They are opportunities to be physically, mentally and spiritually refreshed. Most retreats will provide a balance of times of personal prayer and corporate worship, times to be spiritually encouraged and intellectually stimulated, times to share in conversation and enjoy good healthy food, times to rest and times to engage in activity. A good retreat should be a life-giving holistic experience.

- Focusing on God: In the midst of the busyness of life, we tend to compartmentalise the different aspects of our lives, our spiritual life becoming one of the many things we 'do'. Our times of personal prayer and Bible meditation tend to be squeezed into a few minutes at the beginning or end of the day. Retreat times can help you reconnect with God by opening all of your senses to God's presence and activity within you and around you. This often leads to transformation and a renewed commitment to focus on God in more intentional ways in your daily life.

- Spiritual formation and transformation: At the heart of the Way of Jesus is the invitation to become like little children and unlearn things we have come to take for granted, in order to learn afresh what it means to be fully human, to be a follower of the Rabbi of Nazareth and to deepen our relationship with God and others. Retreats are crucial in this ongoing process of spiritual formation, providing a space in which your spiritual muscles can be stretched and strengthened for the journey ahead. They also provide the content, through themed, 'taught' retreats and courses, to feed you spiritually and intellectually.

- Space to reflect: There are times when we experience big changes in our personal circumstances, whether they relate to family, other relationships or professional life. These are times in which we have more questions than answers. When you find yourself at a crossroad in life and need some distance from it all to make sense of difficult situations or discern the way forward, a retreat will provide space to think, reflect and clarify your thoughts. It can become a time where healing happens, or when you gain new insights into God's will for your life.

- Being in community: One of the most exciting aspects of going on retreat is to be part of a community of people for a few days. At Los Olivos, we have discovered that being community—eating, praying, talking, learning, laughing and sharing our hopes and fears together—

is central to the experience of hospitality. One of the most rewarding experiences in this type of ministry is when a group of ten or twelve or 15 individuals who have never met before come together at the beginning of a week, and, by the end of the week, are no longer a group of individuals but have become a community. They are no longer strangers to each other; they have become friends.

- Doing something you've never done before: Retreats are opportunities to try new things. They could include exploring a new dimension of Christian spirituality, getting creative and having a go at painting, sculpting or cooking exotic food, having a massage, or simply exploring a new area of the country or the world.

- Space to be: Retreat times provide a conducive environment to 'be', and not just 'do'—to *be* in the present moment, aware of God's presence, without distractions and deadlines. This can be a difficult aspect of being on retreat, but equally it is a very liberating one.

- Mentoring and guidance: Most retreat houses offer opportunities to meet with a spiritual director or companion, to share your journey and help you discern where God is, or what God might be saying to you at that given time. Even if you already have a spiritual director back home, meeting with a different one can be a very useful exercise.

- Connecting with nature: Enjoying God's creation is central to many retreat centres. Los Olivos is in the heart of the Sierra Nevada National Park in southern Spain, with many opportunities for mountain walks, bird watching, flower spotting and contemplating God's work through creation. This is true of many retreat centres around the world, where the location, often in a place of outstanding natural beauty, acts as a wonderful backdrop to the retreat itself.

So, whether you are a frequent retreat flier or someone who has never embarked on such a spiritual flight, I hope these ten reasons will encourage you to take time out to reconnect with yourself, with others and with God, through the precious gift of a personal retreat.

Daniel Muñoz is chaplain to the Los Olivos retreat centre in the heart of the Sierra Nevada National Park in Spain. For details of Los Olivos, visit www.haciendalosolivos.org. For details of our BRF Quiet Days, visit www. brfonline.org.uk/events-and-quiet-days or contact BRF on 01865 319700.

Daniel has also written Transformed by the Beloved: A guide to spiritual formation with St John of the Cross. *To order a copy, please see the order form on page 155, or visit www.brfonline.org.uk.*

Recommended reading

Kevin Ball

Why read books? For enjoyment, to be challenged, to learn, to discover? *The Huffington Post*, a US online newspaper, has published some unconventional reasons why you should be reading books.

- Reading can help you relax and sleep better.
- It can keep your brain sharp into old age and may even stave off Alzheimer's.
- Self-help books can ease depression.
- Reading books that engage your emotions can boost your empathy and can even help you cultivate the ability to read the thoughts and feelings of others.

Whatever you think of this list, the survey that BRF ran last year revealed that, for you, reading Christian books is all about helping you to go deeper with your faith. So what books can BRF offer you right now, to help you stay sharp, empathetic and growing?

This year's Advent book is *Longing, Waiting, Believing* by Rodney Holder. Rodney's *New Daylight* notes on 'Our Creator God' in 2012 brought a refreshing look at the positive engagement of contemporary science with the biblical creation accounts. Rodney now brings his scientific insights to bear on the themes of Advent.

For many of us, prayer means speaking words already prepared on a service sheet, a hasty request when life presses in, or saying 'Amen' to someone else's words. But shouldn't prayer be far more than that? To help you discover the 'more', Daniel Wolpert invites you to explore twelve ancient prayer practices in *Creating a Life with God*.

Journalling the Bible aims to help you past the roadblock faced by many of us—struggling to read the Bible. Author Corin Child guides you through 40 exercises to help you start journalling your insights from Bible passages and how they resonate with your faith experience.

You can find more detail about these books and others on the pages that follow and on our website, www.brfonline.org.uk. Keep reading!

Longing, Waiting, Believing
Reflections for Advent, Christmas and Epiphany
Rodney Holder

In the excitement of preparing for Christmas, the traditionally penitential nature of Advent is often overlooked. In BRF's Advent book for 2014, scientist Rodney Holder takes readers from 1 December to 6 January, covering the well-known events of the nativity story while also showing the relevance of the Advent focus on the 'four last things'—death, judgment, heaven and hell—as part of the build-up to celebrating the incarnation. He draws on relevant insights from his years of work at the interface between science and faith. Material for group use is included in the book.

pb, 978 1 84101 756 3, 192 pages, £7.99 (Also available for Kindle)

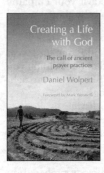

Creating a Life with God
The call of ancient prayer practices
Daniel Wolpert

Here was something that reached down into the core of our dilemma as human beings… something that struck a blow at the evil separating us from loving our brothers and sisters.

Daniel Wolpert invites you to explore twelve ancient prayer practices that have been observed since records of humanity's search for God began. The prayer practices, which include the Jesus Prayer, apophatic prayer, *lectio divina*, body prayer, walking towards God, the examen, journalling and praying in nature, are explored with the help of travelling companions such as Ignatius Loyola, Julian of Norwich, Francis of Assisi and the anonymous author of *The Way of a Pilgrim*.

The journey to discover the true depth of prayer is not instant, warns Daniel, but it is of extreme importance for all who truly want to reach out and find God. *Creating a Life with God* also includes a step-by-step guide to the prayer practices and a model timetable for planning a quiet day or retreat using the book.

pb, 978 0 85746 244 2, 192 pages, £7.99 (Also available for Kindle)

Journalling the Bible
40 creative writing exercises
Corin Child

To grow in faith, becoming a better Christian, is the desire of many people, yet progress can remain elusive. Could the solution lie in writing things down—journalling?

Corin Child makes it easy to start journalling, by offering 40 exercises, arising from Bible passages across scripture. The hope is that by sensing the exhilaration of the biblical writers, you will be stirred to follow their example.

Each reflection is explored through reading the scripture passage and considering the passion of the text, illustrated in many cases by comparisons with other inspiring works, such as famous diaries, literature, songs, films or television programmes. It's then your turn to write, using the helpful journalling template as a guide.

pb, 978 1 84101 736 5, 128 pages, £7.99 (Also available for Kindle)

Timothy Bear and the Baptism Box
12 five-minute stories and simple activities for baptism families
Brian Sears

When his baby sister Teresa is baptised, Timothy Bear learns a lot about what baptism really means—and he discovers that some lessons are easier to learn than others!

Timothy Bear and the Baptism Box contains twelve easy-to-read stories, each exploring a different symbol or action found either in the Church of England baptism service or in the wider baptism journey. The stories lead to the creation of a child's own baptism box.

Baptism symbols and themes include water, oil, the lighted candle, repentance, forgiveness through the sacrifice of Jesus, the meaning of the Trinity, keeping promises, service, perseverance, becoming part of God's family and growing as a Christian. This is an ideal gift for 4–7s.

pb, 978 0 85746 154 4, 96 pages, £6.99

Learning with Foundations21
A seven-week course of study material
Claire Musters

These two study resources, *Prayer* and *Jesus*, provide seven weeks of material for group or individual use. Each week includes an overview session with shorter follow-up sessions through the week, encouraging continuity between one meeting and the next, with questions and activities differentiated for different learning styles, and links to the BRF Foundations21 website (www.foundations21.net).

Prayer
- Week 1: What is prayer?
- Week 2: Prayer in the Bible
- Week 3: Praying Jesus' way
- Week 4: Ways in to prayer
- Week 5: The discipline of prayer
- Week 6: The power of prayer
- Week 7: Praying with others

Jesus
- Week 1: Jesus the Messiah
- Week 2: The divine nature of Jesus
- Week 3: Jesus' humanity
- Week 4: Jesus' teachings
- Week 5: Jesus' 'I am' sayings
- Week 6: Meeting with Jesus
- Week 7: Following Jesus

Prayer: *pb, 978 1 84101 695 5, 80 pages, £4.99*
Jesus: *pb, 978 1 84101 692 4, 80 pages, £4.99*

Both titles are also available as PDF downloads.

To order copies of any of these books, please turn to the order form on page 155, or visit www.brfonline.org.uk.

SUPPORTING BRF'S MINISTRY

As a Christian charity, BRF is involved in seven distinct yet complementary areas.

- **BRF** (www.brf.org.uk) resources adults for their spiritual journey through Bible reading notes, books and Quiet Days. BRF also provides the infrastructure that supports our other specialist ministries.
- **Foundations21** (www.foundations21.net) provides flexible and innovative ways for individuals and groups to explore their Christian faith and discipleship through a multimedia internet-based resource.
- **Messy Church** (www.messychurch.org.uk), led by Lucy Moore, enables churches all over the UK (and increasingly abroad) to reach children and adults beyond the fringes of the church.
- **Barnabas in Churches** (www.barnabasinchurches.org.uk) helps churches to support, resource and develop their children's ministry with the under-11s more effectively .
- **Barnabas in Schools** (www.barnabasinschools.org.uk) enables primary school children and teachers to explore Christianity creatively and bring the Bible alive within RE and Collective Worship.
- **Faith in Homes** (www.faithinhomes.org.uk) supports families to explore and live out the Christian faith at home.
- **Who Let The Dads Out** (www.wholetthedadsout.org) inspires churches to engage with dads and their pre-school children.

At the heart of BRF's ministry is a desire to equip adults and children for Christian living—helping them to read and understand the Bible, explore prayer and grow as disciples of Jesus. We need your help to make an impact on the local church, local schools and the wider community.

- You could support BRF's ministry with a one-off gift or regular donation (using the response form on page 153).
- You could consider making a bequest to BRF in your will.
- You could encourage your church to support BRF as part of your church's giving to home mission—perhaps focusing on a specific area of our ministry, or a particular member of our Barnabas team.
- Most important of all, you could support BRF with your prayers.

If you would like to discuss how a specific gift or bequest could be used in the development of our ministry, please phone 01865 319700 or email enquiries@brf.org.uk.

Whatever you can do or give, we thank you for your support.

BRF has been helping individuals connect with the Bible for over 90 years. We want to support churches as they seek to encourage church members into regular Bible reading.

Order a Bible reading resources pack

This pack is designed to give your church the tools to publicise our Bible reading notes. It includes:

- Sample Bible reading notes for your congregation to try.
- Publicity resources, including a poster.
- A church magazine feature about Bible reading notes.

The pack is free, but we welcome a £5 donation to cover the cost of postage. If you require a pack to be sent outside the UK or require a specific number of sample Bible reading notes, please contact us for postage costs. More information about what the current pack contains is available on our website.

How to order and find out more

- Visit **www.biblereadingnotes.org.uk/for-churches/**
- Telephone BRF on 01865 319700 between 9.15 am and 5.30 pm.
- Write to us at BRF, 15 The Chambers, Vineyard, Abingdon, OX14 3FE

Keep informed about our latest initiatives

We are continuing to develop resources to help churches encourage people into regular Bible reading, wherever they are on their journey. Join our email list at **www.biblereadingnotes.org.uk/helpingchurches/** to stay informed about the latest initiatives that your church could benefit from.

Introduce a friend to our notes

We can send information about our notes and current prices for you to pass on. Please contact us.

ND0314

BRF MINISTRY APPEAL RESPONSE FORM

I want to help BRF by funding some of its core ministries. Please use my gift for:
- ❏ Where most needed ❏ Barnabas Children's Ministry ❏ Foundations21
- ❏ Messy Church ❏ Who Let The Dads Out?

Please complete all relevant sections of this form and print clearly.

Title _____ First name/initials _____ Surname _____

Address _____

_____ Postcode _____

Telephone _____ Email _____

Regular giving

If you would like to give by direct debit, please tick the box below and fill in details:

❏ I would like to make a regular gift of £ _____ per month / quarter / year
(delete as appropriate) by Direct Debit. (Please complete the form on page 159.)

If you would like to give by standing order, please contact Debra McKnight (tel: 01865 319700; email debra.mcknight@brf.org.uk; write to BRF address).

One-off donation

Please accept my special gift of
❏ £10 ❏ £50 ❏ £100 (other) £ _____ by

❏ Cheque / Charity Voucher payable to 'BRF'
❏ Visa / Mastercard / Charity Card
(delete as appropriate)

Name on card _____

Card no. ❏❏❏❏ ❏❏❏❏ ❏❏❏❏ ❏❏❏❏

Start date ❏❏❏   Expiry date ❏❏❏

Security code ❏❏❏

Signature _____ Date _____

❏ I would like to give a legacy to BRF. Please send me further information.

❏ I want BRF to claim back tax on this gift.
(If you tick this box, please fill in gift aid declaration overleaf.)

Please detach and send this completed form to: BRF, 15 The Chambers, Vineyard, Abingdon OX14 3FE.

BRF is a Registered Charity (No.233280)

Bible Reading Fellowship

Please treat as Gift Aid donations all qualifying gifts of money made
today ☐   in the past 4 years ☐   in the future ☐   (tick all that apply)

I confirm I have paid or will pay an amount of Income Tax and/or Capital Gains Tax for each tax year (6 April to 5 April) that is at least equal to the amount of tax that all the charities that I donate to will reclaim on my gifts for that tax year. I understand that other taxes such as VAT or Council Tax do not qualify. I understand the charity will reclaim 25p of tax on every £1 that I give.

☐   My donation does not qualify for Gift Aid.

Signature _____

Date _____

Notes:

1. Please notify BRF if you want to cancel this declaration, change your name or home address, or no longer pay sufficient tax on your income and/or capital gains.

2. If you pay Income Tax at the higher/additional rate and want to receive the additional tax relief due to you, you must include all your Gift Aid donations on your Self-Assessment tax return or ask HM Revenue and Customs to adjust your tax code.

ND0314

BRF PUBLICATIONS ORDER FORM

Please send me the following book(s):

		Quantity	Price	Total
756 3	Longing, Waiting, Believing (R. Holder)	____	£7.99	____
688 7	Creative Prayer Ideas (C. Daniel)	____	£8.99	____
651 1	Mary (A. Jones)	____	£8.99	____
736 5	Journalling the Bible (C. Child)	____	£7.99	____
244 2	Creating a Life with God (D. Wolpert)	____	£7.99	____
584 2	Transformed by the Beloved (D. Muñoz)	____	£6.99	____
154 4	Timothy Bear and the Baptism Box (B. Sears)	____	£6.99	____
695 5	Prayer (C. Musters)	____	£4.99	____
692 4	Jesus (C. Musters)	____	£4.99	____

Total cost of books £ _____
Donation £ _____
Postage and packing £ _____
TOTAL £ _____

POSTAGE AND PACKING CHARGES				
order value	UK	Europe	Surface	Air Mail
£7.00 & under	£1.25	£3.00	£3.50	£5.50
£7.01–£30.00	£2.25	£5.50	£6.50	£10.00
Over £30.00	free	prices on request		

Please complete the payment details below and send with payment to: **BRF, 15 The Chambers, Vineyard, Abingdon OX14 3FE**

Name _____

Address _____

_____ Postcode _____

Tel _____ Email _____

Total enclosed £ _____ (cheques should be made payable to 'BRF')

Please charge my Visa ❏ Mastercard ❏ with £ _____

Card no: ☐☐☐☐ ☐☐☐☐ ☐☐☐☐ ☐☐☐☐ ☐☐☐☐

Expires ☐☐☐☐ Security code ☐☐☐

Signature (essential if paying by card) _____

NEW DAYLIGHT INDIVIDUAL SUBSCRIPTIONS

❏ I would like to take out a subscription myself:

Your name _____

Your address _____

_____ Postcode _____

Tel _____ Email _____

Please send *New Daylight* beginning with the January 2015 / May 2015 /
September 2015 issue: (delete as applicable)

(please tick box)	UK	SURFACE	AIR MAIL
NEW DAYLIGHT	❏ £15.99	❏ £23.25	❏ £25.50
NEW DAYLIGHT 3-year sub	❏ £40.50		
NEW DAYLIGHT DELUXE	❏ £19.80	❏ £30.75	❏ £36.75
NEW DAYLIGHT daily email only	❏ £12.75 (UK and overseas)		

Please complete the payment details below and send with appropriate
payment to: **BRF, 15 The Chambers, Vineyard, Abingdon OX14 3FE**

Total enclosed £ _____ (cheques should be made payable to 'BRF')

Please charge my Visa ❏ Mastercard ❏ with £ _____

Card no: ⬚⬚⬚⬚⬚⬚⬚⬚⬚⬚⬚⬚⬚⬚⬚⬚⬚⬚

Expires ⬚⬚⬚ Security code ⬚⬚⬚

Signature (essential if paying by card) _____

To set up a direct debit, please also complete the form on page 159 and send
it to BRF with this form.

BRF is a Registered Charity

NEW DAYLIGHT GIFT SUBSCRIPTIONS

❏ I would like to give a gift subscription (please provide both names and
addresses:

Your name _____

Your address _____

_____ Postcode _____

Tel _____ Email _____

Gift subscription name _____

Gift subscription address _____

_____ Postcode _____

Gift message (20 words max. or include your own gift card for the recipient)

_____

_____

Please send *New Daylight* beginning with the January 2015 / May 2015 /
September 2015 issue: (delete as applicable)

(please tick box)	UK	SURFACE	AIR MAIL
NEW DAYLIGHT	❏ £15.99	❏ £23.25	❏ £25.50
NEW DAYLIGHT 3-year sub	❏ £40.50		
NEW DAYLIGHT DELUXE	❏ £19.80	❏ £30.75	❏ £36.75
NEW DAYLIGHT daily email only	❏ £12.75 (UK and overseas)		

Please complete the payment details below and send with appropriate
payment to: **BRF, 15 The Chambers, Vineyard, Abingdon OX14 3FE**

Total enclosed £ _____ (cheques should be made payable to 'BRF')

Please charge my Visa ❏ Mastercard ❏ with £ _____

Card no: | | | | | | | | | | | | | | | | | | |

Expires | | | | Security code | | |

Signature (essential if paying by card) _____

To set up a direct debit, please also complete the form on page 159 and send
it to BRF with this form.

DIRECT DEBIT PAYMENTS

Now you can pay for your annual subscription to BRF notes using Direct Debit. You need only give your bank details once, and the payment is made automatically every year until you cancel it. If you would like to pay by Direct Debit, please use the form opposite, entering your BRF account number under 'Reference'.

You are fully covered by the Direct Debit Guarantee:

The Direct Debit Guarantee

- This Guarantee is offered by all banks and building societies that accept instructions to pay Direct Debits.
- If there are any changes to the amount, date or frequency of your Direct Debit, The Bible Reading Fellowship will notify you 10 working days in advance of your account being debited or as otherwise agreed. If you request The Bible Reading Fellowship to collect a payment, confirmation of the amount and date will be given to you at the time of the request.
- If an error is made in the payment of your Direct Debit, by The Bible Reading Fellowship or your bank or building society, you are entitled to a full and immediate refund of the amount paid from your bank or building society.
  - – If you receive a refund you are not entitled to, you must pay it back when The Bible Reading Fellowship asks you to.
- You can cancel a Direct Debit at any time by simply contacting your bank or building society. Written confirmation may be required. Please also notify us.

The Bible Reading Fellowship

Instruction to your bank or building society to pay by Direct Debit

Please fill in the whole form using a ballpoint pen and send to The Bible Reading Fellowship, 15 The Chambers, Vineyard, Abingdon OX14 3FE.

Service User Number: | 5 | 5 | 8 | 2 | 2 | 9 |

Name and full postal address of your bank or building society

To: The Manager	Bank/Building Society
Address	
	Postcode

Name(s) of account holder(s)

Branch sort code

| | | | | | |

Bank/Building Society account number

| | | | | | | | |

Reference

| | | | | | | | |

Instruction to your Bank/Building Society

Please pay The Bible Reading Fellowship Direct Debits from the account detailed in this instruction, subject to the safeguards assured by the Direct Debit Guarantee.
I understand that this instruction may remain with The Bible Reading Fellowship and, if so, details will be passed electronically to my bank/building society.

Signature(s)	
Date	

Banks and Building Societies may not accept Direct Debit instructions for some types of account.

This page is intentionally left blank.